W9-COJ-077

ACCOUNTABILITY

ACCOUNTABILITY

EDWARD A. GALLAWAY

Dorrance & Company ● *Philadelphia*

162317

658.9292
G 165

To my family; the shareholders; and the many fine, loyal workers, both salaried and hourly, who were part of my life for so many years.

Copyright © 1975 by Edward A. Gallaway
All Rights Reserved
ISBN 0-8059-2236-9
Printed in the United States of America

Preface

Accountability is a true story about a youth who entered the industrial world at age eighteen in one of the big three auto companies and progressed from one of the lowest paid hourly jobs to become one of the top executives in a multi-million-dollar operation. He retired after thirty-eight and a half years at age fifty-six. In this book he expresses his dissatisfaction with the lack of accountability on the part of the company's upper echelon.

Introduction

I am fully aware that writing a book regarding my life with one of the three big auto companies will have very limited appeal to readers who believe that sex and phony characters are necessary to sell a book. However, to readers who think that truth is stranger than fiction it will have some appeal. It will be a welcome change to readers who are tired of reading phony fiction and want to read a true life story. The newspapers today are filled with automobile stories, often by writers who are merely expressing their opinions. When I read these articles it is easy to recognize the writers who know very little about producing automobiles. My duties as a production executive were no different from those of any other production executive. Many excellent executives in the Chrysler Corporation will never get the chance to make use of their ability while the present top executives remain in their present position. Just remember $11 billion in sales, second highest in the history of the corporation, resulting in a $52 million-dollar loss in 1974. No one is capable of giving a satisfactory answer to stockholders. None of our competitors went from $4.80 per share to - $.92 a share in the same period, a total loss of $5.72 per share.

The first quarter for 1975 has been announced, the losses continue, and to me the future of a great company is getting darker by the hour. The early chapters of the book cover my activity before my employment with Chrysler and up through my first twenty years with Chrysler. I have recorded the highlights of those years.

This book will show my activity during the war years. (I did not serve in the armed forces.) I have four sons; three have served in the armed forces, the other is only fifteen years old. Two of my sons served in foreign countries.

In the later chapters covering 1957 through 1974, my motive is to arouse the stockholders of any company to watch for the *accountability* that establishes a company as either well managed or poorly managed and to be aware of the action that must be taken to prevent complete failure. Therefore, those years will be covered in detail by year.

Trenton Engine Plant is the largest machining facility in the Chrysler Corporation. It is one of three engine plants that supply all of the passenger-car and truck engines installed in all our assembly plants in the United States and Canada. Trenton Engine is a key plant that produces all the large V/8 engines, both passenger car and trucks, also about 70 percent of all the six-cylinder engines used in cars and trucks built in the United States and Canada.

This book describes upper-echelon activities with regard to Trenton Engine Plant, where I was assigned for eighteen years. In 1974, with sales in excess of $11 billion, resulting in losses of $52 million, it is only reasonable to believe that the *accountability* of the top officers wasn't any better in other plants than it was at Trenton Engine Plant.

Edward A. Gallaway
September 1975

Chapter 1

It was Monday, March 31, 1975, a day I will always remember. The day started out as one of decision, a major decision in the life of a man who had been making decisions for others most of his life; now he must make a decision that would affect himself for the rest of his life. I had walked from my parking spot that morning through the plant to my office asking myself whether I should take early retirement or not. The papers were not signed yet; I could still change my mind. As I came through the plant, several people greeted me with "Good morning, boss" or "Good morning. Hope you changed your mind about retiring." My emotions were all mixed up. I entered my office, unlocked my desk, and sat in my chair, gazing out of the window at the employees working on the V/8 assembly line. Today was the deadline—the papers had to be signed today. Why was I even considering retiring today? Only six months previously hadn't I been the master of ceremonies at our semi-annual retirement party? When anyone would ask, "When are you going to retire?", I would answer that fifty-six years old was too young to retire—sure I had thirty eight years of service, but that only puts me in my prime; my plans call for two to four years yet. As I sat there staring out of the office window my mind was reviewing the years 1972, '73 and '74.

No shareholder who knew the facts would say that I had been treated fairly during those years. In 1972 there had been an incentive compensation pot of $13 million to divide among 1,400 bonus-roll executives. The bonus was to compensate executives such as myself to make up for the fact that we received no overtime pay, no premium pay, no cost-of-living

1

allowance, and low salaries. The $13 million was split up with a few crumbs dribbling down to plant executives. Not one plant executive who had anything to do with production had received sufficient bonus to pay for his overtime—none was satisfied. The big money went to the top officers and their staffs. We who had generated this money had been almost ignored; only those who had soft spots and produced nothing had been well compensated. Nothing was ever published in the way of *accountability* to justify this type of distribution. 1973 was a repeat of 1972, only there was a bigger pot to share, $19 million—the rich got richer. Down in the plants, where the executives had to generate the incentive compensation pot, we again got the crumbs. 1974 started out as a repeat of 1973; we worked overtime continuously and received none of the fringe benefits that non-bonus-roll executives received. We were hopeful that the incentive compensation committee would recognize that their method of distribution was very unjust. If they had compared their award with those given by their competitors to the plant executives doing the same kind of work, the distribution might have been different.

1972 and 1973 had been morale wreckers to plant executives, but 1974 was the real backbreaker; as for myself I worked 980 hours of overtime. We had run overtime through 1974 models with thousands upon thousands of cars unsold. We started building 1975 models on overtime to add to the already overstocked sales bank. This continued through October and then the higher officers realized that cars weren't selling. The fourth quarter was going to be bad; it would wipe out all profits made in the first three quarters and then some. Drastic action had to be taken—stop the stock plan, eliminate the cost-of-living allowance for all non-union employees, no merit increase, no bonus, take away the employees' holiday pay, make the salaried workers use up their 1975 vacations, cut the bonus executives' pay 15 percent for January for those making $2,500 or more per month, and do the same for February and March except for those who earned under

$2,500. My pay was $2,455 per month, so my cut was 15 percent in January, 10 percent in February, and 10 percent in March. The controller had told me this could go on indefinitely. Most of my executives, even without their cost-of-living allowance, were making more money than I was. The higher officers weren't interested in making sure that we executives at plant level were justly compensated; every one of us was held *accountable* for our contribution to the success of the corporation, but after $11 billion in sales resulted in $52 million in losses, they made damn sure we received more than our share of the loss. The next move affected all shareholders: the small dividend was eliminated (stock had dropped 75 percent in two years).

So as I sat there watching the line run, my mind was asking the question, *What can I do to reorganize the upper echelon so that $11 billion in sales will result in millions in profit?* Mismanagement by the top officers stood out like a sore thumb. Their proxy statement and annual report had satisfied very few of the stockholders. The dissatisfied stockholders could take action and turn this corporation around—why not a book outlining the many areas of mismanagement? Would the shareholders be concerned enough to try to save this automobile company, increase their share value, and get a dividend for their investment? Perhaps if they knew a little about me, if my story could convince the shareholders that what they expect from Chrysler can be accomplished only by the shareholders' organized aggressive action, they will act to save their investment.

Since my shares were a major part of my life savings, it was only natural that dividends and stock value played an important role in my retirement plans. Now, after thirty-eight and a half years, because of mismanagement of top corporate executives, my 1,700-share investment was worth about $17,000. Can anyone imagine a Ford or General Motors executive being manufacturing general superintendent in a multi-million-dollar operation for nine years and then being offered a retirement of less than $1,000 per month? I can't and no other shareholder who knows the facts would understand this type of compensation. But our top officers have a way of doing things differently from General Motors and Ford. They could lose $52 million while sales were $11 billion, second best in corporate history. It must be clear to the shareholders by this time that our country-club officers, (and they all had membership paid for by the corporation in exclusive country clubs) were spending their time and our money, doing nothing with regard to running a profitable automobile company. There was a complete lack of *accountability* for the way the company ran in 1974. Our top officers were well compensated for their dismal showing, considering the $52 million loss for which they found all kinds of excuses except mismanagement or their own culpability.

As these thoughts passed through my mind it became obvious to me that this great corporation could be turned around, but it would take someone with guts enough to bring the facts to the attention of its owners—shareholders such as myself. I am willing to give up the position I worked so hard and so long to get, willing to do my part to motivate the shareholders by writing a history of myself to get them to realize as I do that all is not lost, that united we shareholders must stand, that divided we will surely fall. The time to start is *now*.

Chapter 2

Life for me began on September 17, 1918, in the lumber camp in Cheboygan County, Michigan. The birth certificate says that I arrived on the 19th but my mother, who is still living, insists it was the 17th, and she should know because it wasn't a normal birth. I was in the process of being born feet first; the doctor had informed my father that he could save

4

the mother or the baby. He was instructed to save the mother. Since I was the fourth child, it would have been a bad decision to save the baby and then have four motherless children. God was watching over us that day: I came feet first and we both survived. That was the beginning of my existence. Ours was a life of hard times and hard work, and the reward was food, clothes, and a roof over our heads—nothing more. My father was a carpenter by trade, also a teamster in the lumber camps and a farmer. He worked hard at all these jobs to try to make a living for his family, which eventually totaled seven children. Ten years later, in 1928, we were living on a farm in Livingston County near Brighton, Michigan. My father had bought this farm so he could put us to work to support ourselves (he was a firm believer that hard work never hurt anyone). Work assignments were issued to each one of us. It seemed to me that once you became old enough to go to school, you were old enough to be given full-time work on the farm. We were held fully *accountable* for the tasks assigned to us, no excuses were acceptable for failure, and all-out effoot was a must. A leather strap hanging on the kitchen door knob was put to use whenever he felt we were forgetful or lax. It was used quite often. He ruled by arousing fear—the only way, he thought. That method of leadership worked in those days and it certainly got the full measure from all in our family.

Our work day was daylight to dark; Sunday was church day. We always went to church on Sunday. The everyday chores consisted of milking cows and feeding horses, hogs, chickens, then cleaning the stables; all this usually took about four hours. We had a rather easy day, we had plenty to eat, and while we didn't have the best of clothes, my mother worked hard to keep us clean. Since I was only ten years old one might wonder what work I was capable of doing. During the summer I was up at dawn and getting the cattle in from the pasture so we could milk them before breakfast. The dew would be heavy on the grass and the sun just breaking over the horizon. We kids always went barefoot during the summer—shoes had to

5

saved for winter. I could stand on a nail keg and harness horses (we had no tractors); pulling weeds, hoeing thistles, feeding hogs and chickens were some of my everyday duties. I also remember following my father while he was cultivating corn and potatoes. My job was to uncover any plants that he might cover with loose dirt. He usually knew when dirt would cover a hill of corn. I would be trailing him by fifteen or twenty feet and he would stop the horse and watch to see if I uncovered the corn. If I failed to see the dirt, he would take me by the ear back to the hill of corn, show it to me and sometimes boot me in the rear when I bent over to uncover it. He held me *accountable* to uncover any corn that was covered and he accepted nothing less.

Chapter 3

A land-developing company called The Capitol Land Company was buying hundreds of acres of property in this area. They were working on a project called Woodland Golf and Country Club. They purchased part of our farm because they were building a dam which would create a large lake and would flood part of our property. We sold this portion of the property on a second land contract. The dam was completed and as a result Woodland Lake was born. It is located just northeast of Brighton, Michigan. The crash came in 1929, the development company went broke, and we received our flooded property back while my father was still buying the farm. The depression hit and farming alone could not supply the money to keep up the payments. In 1931 or 1932 my father was forced to sell his equity and move out. He received a small amount of cash and fifty acres on Drummond Island in the Upper Peninsula. Today many fine homes line the lake front on the northeast side of Woodland Lake. Like many others', our dreams had been destroyed by the depression. We rented another farm in Livingston County located on Kensington Road, which is now a part of Kensington Park. During the depression years we lived off what we could produce on the farm. My father did get a small amount of welfare aid.

As a farm youth I always had work to do before and after school. Sometimes during harvest time I was not allowed to go to school because I was needed to help with the farm work. In spite of this my grades were excellent. In 1934 I graduated from grade school with honors. The Civilian Conservation Corps had been established and my older brother James was in one of the camps at Houghton Lake. At my father's request I enlisted. The minimum age was eighteen, but by lying about my age I was accepted. The teacher at the grade school I attended heard about my enlistment (she thought I had great potential) and made it her business to visit my father. She requested of him that I be kept out of the Civilian Conservation Corps and continue in school. He explained to her that the twenty-five dollar check that would be coming in monthly was sorely needed to help support the family. My education could be continued at a later date. I was a member of Company 1666, located at Ludington, Michigan, for twenty-one months. I received five dollars per month, my parents received twenty-five; room, board, and clothing were furnished. The Civilian Conservation Corps camps were excellent for disciplining and straightening out boys who had never worked or had never been held accountable for anything. They were a vacation for farm youths who were used to hard work. The C.C.C. camps did a lot for the nation—they made men out of boys.

Work was becoming available in 1936, and pay was better at other jobs. In order to be released, one had to have a job, so my brother wrote me a letter saying that work was available at the Ford Motor Company, where he was then employed and where he continued to be employed until March 31, 1975, when he retired. I showed the letter to my commanding officer and received an honorable discharge in March 1936. I received reference recommendations from the educational director, commanding officer, staff supervisor, and personal work supervisor. All references outlined many of the activities I had excelled in during my length of service; all ended by saying that I would be a valuable asset in any field that I might choose to follow and to any concern that might enlist my services. I lost all these recommendations by answering ads in the *News* or *Free Press*, even though when enclosing a recommendation I would send a self-addressed, stamped envelope asking that it be returned; none was ever returned. Up to that period in life I considered myself extremely fortunate. I had close calls and three times by the grace of God I was saved. While bathing I had been pulled out of School Lake after going down for the last time. My sister Dorothy saved me—she was the only one who could swim. She saw me disappear beneath the water and got me out and I was saved by artificial respiration. Twice while in the C.C.C. Camp I had been in severe automobile accidents, once while riding in the back of a dump truck which rolled over and the second while riding in the back of an army truck which was struck broadside by another auto. Many men had been injured on both occasions, but other than a few bruises I was lucky.

Chapter 4

At seventeen and a half I was too young to get a factory job and there was not enough work on the farm on Kensington Road to keep the whole family busy, so about the middle of April, 1936, I started out to answer an ad in Oxford, Michigan, for a farm hand.

Hitchhiking or walking was my only means of getting there. By walking to Oxford and thumbing a ride, then walking and thunbing another ride, I was getting close, but "close" was as far as I got. The next thing I knew there were voices that were not familiar... I was in Pontiac General Hospital. I was regaining consciousness, doctors and nurses were around my bed and I heard someone say, "Do you think we should operate?" Then someone said, "Do you detect a stutter?" Operate? Stutter? Where am I?... opening my eyes and looking around ... what a feeling! A nurse came to my bed; in answer to my questions she said, "You are in Pontiac General Hospital, you have been in a serious accident, and we have your bed slanted so as to keep the blood out of your head."

Meanwhile, my brother, who was working at Ford, had arrived at work and one of his co-workers asked him if he had seen an article in the *Free Press* about an accident, and was that Gallaway any relation to him? My brother hadn't read the paper but the more he thought about it the more it bothered him. About 10:00 A.M. he decided to investigate. He got a pass, went to his car, and drove to the farm. Seeing that I wasn't there, he asked mother, "Where's Ed?" "Job hunting," she replied. "He was hiking to Oxford, Michigan, in answer to an ad; that was a couple of days ago and we haven't heard from him since."

My brother called my dad. "Dad, you and Mom get ready, we are going to Pontiac General Hospital. Ed has been in an accident and is in critical condition there." Mother fainted.

When I came to, my mother, father, and brother were at the hospital. As soon as they were allowed, they came in to see me. It was a tearful reunion. The man who had picked me up had missed a curve near Lake Orion—it was raining and muddy. The car had rolled over twice and hit a tree, and on the second roll I went out through the top. The mud on my jacket showed that I had landed on the back of my head and shoulders. The injuries were bruises to neck and shoulders and a severe concussion to the back of the head.

My memory of the hike from the time I left home until I woke up in the hospital has always been a complete blank. My recovery was quite rapid. In June I was hired at the Walled Lake ice house. My job was to use an electrical hoist to pull and store blocks of ice, then refill the containers. I worked two or three days and then I got a job at the Vagabond Coach Company in New Hudson. The same day I went to work building house trailers, the man who took my job at the ice house was electrocuted. The hoist had shorted out. I felt the good Lord was still on my side.

My job at the coach company consisted of building the side and trunk doors for two trailers in a ten-hour period. This included fitting, hanging, and installing a metal trim around each door, and putting latches and locks on. I always managed to finish just as they were pulling the trailer out the door. My pay was thirty cents per hour, ten hours a day, six days a week; in short, eighteen dollars a week. We furnished our own tools except for power saws. My job was to complete the door work on two trailers per day. I was held *accountable* for both quality and quantity. It was a helluva big work load by today's standards, even for a young lad who was used to hard work.

I became eighteen years old on September 17, 1936. I remember the day well because my dad took my check to cash in the grocery store in Brighton. He promised to bring me back some of my pay so that I could celebrate my birthday. When he returned I was upstairs getting dressed. He came up and wished me a happy birthday and handed me fifty cents. "After paying for the groceries," he said, "there was only one dollar left, so I'm splitting it with you."

James, my older brother working at Ford, was keeping his eyes open for places that were hiring. He noticed a lineup on McGraw Street in front of the DeSoto plant. I changed shifts at the coach company so that I could be in that line early next morning and each day, if necessary. My application was accepted the week following my eighteenth birthday. I went on the payroll September 28, 1936. As a material handler at sixty-five cents an hour, I was in my glory.

Chapter 5

The education that my father said could continue at a later date now began. The first couple of months were routine. Work was hard, but in comparison with other jobs I had had, the pay was good. After six years of difficult times, anyone who could get work made every effort to hold on to it. Your only security was working hard enough to satisfy the management.

My first assignment was in the paint shop. I was big and strong, six feet tall, and weighed 190 pounds with no fat. Unloading the prime paint oven and loading the paint spray color line was fast and hot work. The cement on the floor was hard on tender feet. The spray line conveyor belt ran fast enough to handle all the material from the prime oven. It was just a matter of hustling enough to keep up with both conveyors and not get burnt. Some of the hooks had excessive paint on them and would actually be smoking. I had to change hooks when transferring from oven to spray conveyor. There was no personal relief. You had to come to work prepared to work four hours straight. My superintendent was happy with my performance. He told me there was a better job in the future for me but replacing me was going to be tough, and I would have to wait until a satisfactory replacement was available. He was true to his word; about two months later I was moved into the metal-polishing room. The pay was $1.05 per hour—boy, was I happy to get a break like this! $8.40 per day—it was hard to believe! The paint in those days was lacquer. The procedure to prepare finished sheet metal was prime, water sand, spray color, water sand, polish, touchup, and O.K. The finished work was stored to shipped downstairs to car assembly. Metal polishing was done by a motor similar to a disc grinder, the difference being we used sheepskin discs instead of sandpaper. There were five men on each side of the line. Between us ran a moving conveyor with bucks carrying all the hoods, fenders, and other materials that had to be polished. On one side of the line there would be two roughers, two finishers, and a touch-up man. New men like me were always started as roughers. Polish flew in all directions. It was a dirty job and one was filthy by the end of the shift. A shower was available; I used it each night and changed clothing before going home. I developed corns and callouses on my feet due to shifting my weight from one foot to the other on the hard cement: in metal-polishing I put my weight either all on one foot or on the other. I could hardly walk by the end of the day.

There was some talk of union organization; I listened but did not join until shortly before the 1937 sit-down strike. Once I joined, however, I decided I should be held *accountable* to do my part to make the organization successful. When we shut down the conveyors and announced that the strike was on, we immediately took over the gates and started escorting management personnel out of the plant. Many of the oldest card-carrying members went over the fence. Our number left in the plant was much smaller than we wanted anyone to believe or know.

I was driving a 1933 V/8 Ford and volunteered to haul food into the plant to feed the strikers. The food was prepared in a hall on Maybury Grand near Michigan Avenue. This was one of the food sources. We were afraid to let many men out because we knew that, once out of the plant, they would not return. Our number was already too small—we could not let it get any smaller. We all knew that the active members would be the first ones discharged in the event the strike was broken. When the strike ended we marched out of the plant. We were claiming a majority of the employees belonged to the union. If that were true most of them were home, because we had less than a hundred to march out that day. Sometime later I received a medal from the union for my participation in the 1937 sit-down strike.

Chapter 6

In 1938 we had the usual layoff for model change. Unemployment checks for a single person came to sixteen dollars a week for a total of sixteen weeks. The paint shop changed to synthetic enamel paint; this eliminated polishing and reduced the number of employees by quite a large number. I was transferred to the press plant and demoted back to material handling. The work force was reduced, and I was laid off quite early in the season. I took a job as a farm hand near Oxford. It was a big dairy farm, where I drove a tractor and milked cows—there were about sixty of them. Wages were thirty-five dollars a month, plus room and board. The hours were from 4:00 a.m. to 9:00 p.m., with every third Sunday off. There were three of us hired men.

I quit this job when the owner refused to give me my dinner when I failed to hear the dinner bell. The direction of the wind and the noise of the tractor had made the bell hard to hear, and I had no watch. He said I should have been able to tell time by the position of the sun. I didn't go back to the field but instead went to my car and drove home. At the end of the month I went back to collect my pay. He tried to hire me back with a raise in pay, but I wanted no part of him or his farm.

Then I was called back to my material-handling job in the stamp plant. I wanted to make more money, so I accepted a job as a power hammerer's helper. Hammer operators were the highest-paid men doing hourly work in the stamp plant: $1.35 per hour, with helpers paid $.85 per hour. This job did require a lot of overtime, as I recall, but weekend work was only straight time.

During my lunch period I would practice metal polishing. When they started hiring metal polishers for the main plant, I asked for and was given a tryout. I passed the test and was transferred the next week. It was damn hard work but the pay was better: $1.10 per hour.

13

I bought a new Dodge, a wonderful car. During the fall of 1939 I married Martha. I also was elected district committee-man for the second-floor area of the plant, collecting dues and handling grievances. It was a thankless job, with no time allowed off the job during working hours. When called upon to represent someone I always had to go back to my operation and catch up on work that had piled up while I was away on union business. In addition to all the extra time I spent trying to keep members paid up, I still had to pay my own dues.

Membership meetings were held on Sundays at some hall. Not many members would show up unless some vital issue that directly affected them was going to be discussed that day. Later on we tried to improve attendance with free beer, which helped some.

In 1940 I decided to further my education by going to night school. I enrolled in a course called Methods Engineering, which met two nights a week and also had plenty of home-work. We took time studies and then worked them out, learned to read a slide rule and all types of gauges. After getting a diploma for the course, I continued on and received a diploma for blueprint reading. In December 1940 our first son, Edward Thomas, was born.

One Monday morning I was checking on dues collections with one of my line stewards. There were six such stewards in my district. Collecting dues was like pulling teeth. You had to chase some of the workers to the bar where they cashed their checks in order to collect their dues. They were the ones who bellyached the most and were the hardest to collect from. One fellow worker wanted to know what had happened at the Sunday membership meeting.

"Why the hell didn't you attend?" I asked. "Then you'd know."

He responded with the remark, "You can't take it, can you?"

"I can take any thing you can dish out," was all I said, but it was enough. Word spread throughout the plant that there was going to be a big fight in the parking lot after work. I had no desire to fight, but it was the topic of the day, and as the day wore on it became evident that there would be a fight. I received a lot of advice that day on how long-winded and what a good athlete my opponent was. Since there was no honorable alternative, I planned my strategy.

The parking lot was jammed. Many stood on the tops of their cars. I sent word that I would not fight on company property, so the site was moved to the alley just outside the parking lot. At the end of the shift I took my time washing up and was one of the last out of the plant. I moved my car out of the parking lot, parked on the side street, and headed for the alley, where he was waiting for me. The fight would be fair—the crowd would be sure of that. I was wearing a pair of leather gloves that had seams on them. I asked for and received his permission to wear them during the fight. I fought a defensive fight, letting him dance around and throw punches; I would ward them off and wait for an opening. He fought in flurries; I tied him up whenever he got in close. He hit me on the side of the head and in the chest, but he made the mistake of getting in close and missing with a right hand—he was wide open. I caught him with a short right hand in the mouth, then a left and another right. He went down, his mouth and face bleeding, then got up slowly, but once on his feet started swinging wildly. The bloodthirsty crowd was hollering at me to finish him. Then a squad car drove up and someone yelled, "Police!" The crowd scattered. The fight was over. About a week later I resigned my position as district committeeman.

Chapter 7

After Pearl Harbor the company stopped making auto-mobiles, converting to war materials. I worked at DeSoto during the day and as a mill operator at night: 7:00 a.m. to 3:30 p.m. at DeSoto, and 4:00 p.m. to 12:30 a.m. at the tool shop. After a couple of months of this I quit the tool shop. We were tooling to build the Bofors anti-aircraft gun casings, single-barrel for the Army, double-barrel for the Navy. Suddenly we had a lot of equipment that very few people knew how to operate.

I received my notice to report for a physical prior to induction into the armed services. I passed the physical and was put in the Navy pool. When called I would serve in the Navy.

I had been offered two jobs as time-study man at other companies. In the gun plant I started out as a machine operator and in about a month was promoted to job setter. I was one of the few who could read height gauges and blueprints. I was working twelve hours a day job-setting at $1.25 an hour, with time and a half for overtime. The operating manager (we will call him Mr. George) asked me to take a job as a supervisor. We couldn't come to an agreement on wages—he offered $250 per month; I wanted $300. He finally agreed to this, but when I got my check it was for $275.

In December 1942 our second son, Dennis Patrick, was born. I received my notice that my military status was 1-A, subject to call within twenty-four hours. The company appealed the classification because of my blueprint and methods engineering training. I was declared essential and given an occupational deferment classification 2-B, subject to review every six months. My classification changed every six months until 1945.

All of the DeSoto plant was producing war materials. We hired a large number of female employees on the wing job, about ten women to every man. In the gun plant where I worked the ratio was about 30 percent. I started out as a foreman of the profile machining line. Later the Natco multiple drill line and the file line were added to my group. At a later date the 100-G inspection department was also added

16

to my responsibilities. My number of employees was four times more than any other foreman in the gun plant. I was held *accountable,* but added money never accompanied the added responsibilities. The additional compensation was always promised but never delivered.

In spite of this I liked the challenge and enjoyed my work. My superiors had a great deal of confidence in me, which I especially appreciated. Work standards were very loose and tools were plentiful. Employees were in excess. It seemed to me the number of parts produced was important, but the cost was not. I do know that many times I had two men on a machine when only one was needed, yet whenever I questioned this, it was explained that we were on a cost-plus basis. We paid the price at a later date for lack of efficiency in those days. The habits of the workers had to change radically when DeSoto started to build automobiles again and efficiency and performance became the name of the game.

During the war years, I helped out on our farm during the planting and harvesting seasons. Tires and gas were rationed, but I received an extra allotment because of my farm work. A lot of other items were rationed, but I don't recall that we encountered any real hardship as a result of the rationing. When I accepted the supervisory position, I was put on the third shift, 10:30 p.m. to 6:30 a.m.. After a short time I was transferred to the second shift and then to the first. All changes of shifts were at my own request. It seemed incredible that I couldn't get a raise, even though two men were needed to replace me on the second shift when I insisted on filling an opening on the first shift. The day-shift position was much easier and home life more pleasant.

As I have stated, there were many women available during the war years; temptations were always prevalent. I was no angel but my marriage did survive.

Bowling was a favorite sport, but a sport which I think is a loser is betting on the horses. One of my job setters came to me one day in late 1943 and asked me to give him a buck for a good double he had picked out. I had never bet on a horse race, never had the slightest idea of what they paid or how to pick them. He called me that night and said we had won. Bookie odds on a daily double then were one hundred to one; the daily double paid about $350. My share of the bet was $101. I often wished I had lost that bet because he came back for a buck every day for a couple of months, but we never won again. In later years when I played the horses and went to the track, my losses at the end of the year were always greater than my winnings. However, losing money always put me in the position of having to earn more money. In order to support my family, I worked harder for promotions in the plant, took part-time jobs in machine shops during the week and tended bar on the weekends. We borrowed from all the finance companies, sometimes from one to pay the other. We also had several charge accounts at department stores. Martha worked part-time and I baby-sat; we were always *accountable* for our debts, and we always managed to have excellent credit ratings. Our home, a new one purchased in 1942, was kept in good condition; the children were clean and healthy—we were average people in a fast-moving society.

Chapter 8

In April 1945 our first daughter, Margaret Ellen, was born. We were very hopeful that our new arrival would be a girl—our wishes were granted. My military status was changed from 2-B back to 1-A, subject to immediate call. The company appealed the 1-A classification, but this time they lost the appeal. I received my "greetings" from Uncle Sam to report for induction on August 16, 1945. VE day had come and gone; my assignment would be to the Army, destination Japan. We made all the necessary preparations. I took leave of my job at the plant on August 1, and there was a farewell party held for me. With a four-month-old baby and two small sons, my wife was quite upset. I think she felt if I went to Japan I would never return. While I would never admit it, I felt the same way. After the atomic bomb fell in August and Japan surrendered, the draft board phoned instructing me not to report on the sixteenth or until further notice. You can't imagine how we felt. It was a great relief to know that the family would remain together. It shows that many of the things that worry people the most never happen.

I returned to work on the Monday following VJ Day. VJ Day meant immediate change back to auto production. Clearing the plant of the equipment used for military material was a large project. The big backlog of auto requirements increased the urgency to start building automobiles.

We did not need salesmen—all we needed were order takers and service facilities. Each dealer had a long list of customers waiting for a new automobile. Their motto was first come, first served. Of course that was not the way it worked: if you were in a position to give $500 extra, your name moved up to the top of the list fast. I had a very close friend who was a part owner of a dealership and who confided in me, so I knew what was happening. My name was near the top of the list, and every time I would ask him when my car was coming through he would check the list. There were always more names between me and the top than when I first gave him the order. I wouldn't pay extra, so I couldn't get a car. My new car came through another dealership about the middle of 1948. Our top executives knew of this black market, but they took very little action to stop it. We lost a lot of good customers because of this practice.

While clearing the plants of government equipment we spared no expense, mainly because it was government expense. I went on special assignment in August 1945 collecting special fixtures and tools to send to the government warehouse with the machines. My job ended December 15, 1945, and I was demoted back to my original classification of

19

metal polisher. Before the war Chrysler seldom promoted from within, but after the war they decided maybe some of the wartime supervisors were capable of being good peacetime supervisors. We still had the same operating manager. My name was submitted to him for consideration for a foreman position in the metal shop. He came to talk to me and asked if I was interested in returning to supervision.

"Heaven knows we need strong supervisors," he said. "We have enough weak ones now and someone has to carry them—we don't need any more of those. There will always be problems, but remember, most people make most of their own problems." With that he slapped me on the shoulder and said, "Good luck." I don't recall talking to him again.

In June 1946 I was returned to supervision on the second shift in the sheet-metal finishing department. We accepted sheet metal from the stamp plant and prepared it for the paint shop. There were seventy-five men on the second shift; gas welders, metal polishers, metal finishers, spot welders, multiple spot welders, and conveyor loaders made up the bulk of manpower. I was held *accountable* for the productivity of each man. Since I have always been of the opinion that inspirational leadership has advantages over browbeating types of leadership, I made an effort to use this method throughout my career.

Chapter 9

In 1947 housing shortages developed, and many firms started to build factory-assembled homes. Adirondack Log Cabin Company of New York was one of these. They were advertising for distributors in my area. I decided to form a company and build homes. I bought a set of books of mathematics, including calculus and trigonometry. I studied these for some time each day. I had to get more experience in sales and home building. I took a real estate sales examination and scored 98 percent on the test. I became a part-time licensed salesman with C. Shuett Realty. I bought books on building codes and corporate law; they were quite complex, but I studied them when time permitted. Understand, this was all being done in the mornings, since I was supervising the sheet metal department at DeSoto on the second shift. I continued in this capacity during my venture into the housing business. The company we formed was called Choice Homes, Inc. We retained an attorney who handled the paper work for the Michigan incorporation process. We were incorporated for $50,000 with $12,000 paid in. We had a franchise with the Adirondack Log Cabin Company of New York to be their distributors for most of Michigan. The market was adequate; we intended to get started and then sell stock. I was elected president; then the hard work and problems began. We had a log cabin on display in the builders' show. Adirondack Log Cabin Company provided us with literature and prices F.O.B. New York. I flew to New York with our treasurer and reviewed our source.

Adirondack had a great sales promotion going covering a number of states. We had an overabundance of customers—many had made deposits on homes and cabins. We were skeptical about promises of delivery dates and freight costs. Big business builders were moving in to shut out factory-built homes, hitting small companies such as ours especially hard. Working through the F.H.A. and the township and county offices where we had to obtain our building permits, we had our specifications checked and rejected in some townships because of double joists, rafters, and studs on 16" centers. All sorts of reasons were manufactured to keep from issuing permits. All resort buildings were ruled out. G.I. homes must come first, a priority with which we were in agreement.

We were working hard and getting an education fast. We had an office on Grand River Avenue. Many of our would-be customers wanted us to build on their lots, but when I checked with the F.H.A. the agency would reject the lot. That meant no financial assistance. A conventional builder could start a building with a down payment from the customer on an F.H.A.-approved lot. He could get a draw when the basement was completed, another draw when the framework was up, and another draw when the plumbing and plastering were done. In other words, he used very little of his own money, if any. Not so with pre-fab buildings—we were fast running out of money.

The Adirondack Log Cabin Company came out with another big promotion in *Look* magazine. The new building was called the 1948 Look House. It was to be built "on your lot complete for $7,500." It didn't include a basement, but a utility room, refrigerator, and stove were provided. We made a trip to New York and looked at the new model. It would sell, but could it be built for that price, and what would the profit margin be? That was the big question. We decided to take one. With *Look* magazine featuring the house, we thought maybe we could sell it to customers who would erect it on their own lots themselves. We ran into all kinds of problems erecting the model. The code called for copper in the plumbing, but all the copper tubing had been bought up. We had to sub-contract most of the work to established builders with union labor. When the house was finished we had more invested in it than we were allowed to sell it for.

Thousands of people viewed the house model in Southfield Township on the corner of Greenview and Eight Mile Road. Thousands of people wanted to place orders. We took names and addresses but no deposits; at the time we were holding deposits on other types of buildings. The treasurer got disgusted and quit, as did the recording secretary. I took on both extra jobs. We decided to return all deposits and pay up all creditors. That meant disposing of some property and finishing some homes that we had just started. Each of us took a sixty-six percent loss in our initial investment. We could have declared bankruptcy, but we felt we were *accountable,* so we took the loss and chalked it up to experience. There is nothing that compares with practical experience. Had we known as much about home building in 1947 as we did in 1949, things would have been different. We could have been a success.

Chapter 10

In 1949 our second daughter, Marilyn Elizabeth, was born. Our children now were four: two boys and two girls.

Chrysler Corporation had four major cars: Chrysler, De-Soto, Dodge, and Plymouth. Each one, of course, had several different models. Our operating personnel was held to a minimum. DeSoto had a president, an operating manager, a master mechanic, a chief inspector, and a general super-intendent of production. They were held *accountable* and were well compensated. The general headquarters staff at Highland Park was very small compared to the burden it ac-cumulated in later years. DeSoto consisted of the main assembly plant on McGraw, the press plant on McGraw, and the body and engine plant on Warren Avenue.

As a foreman in the metal shop on the second shift, I had 140 employees, who were always setting the pace. I could get the best out of my manpower, no one ever disputed that. I wasn't given an increase in salary to compensate for the heavy workload, but a foreman was added to help me. An additional foreman was also added to the first shift. I should have been entitled to the first shift, which I requested. The general superintendent agreed but said my new foreman had to be broken in before he would move me.

After two months I was given my chance on the first shift at which time productivity increased throughout the metal shop, but this time the second shift fell apart. I was asked to take over the second shift again as general foreman and accepted the assignment. After two years of running the second shift with good performance, I realized I was helping the second shift superintendent to look very good—this could go on indefinitely. I had to get out of this somehow.

About 1950 the Warren Avenue body shop was put into action. It was very poorly managed; many of the managers came from the Kaiser Frazer plant at Willow Run, which was rapidly going out of business. Why these managers were selected will always remain a big question mark to me. Had they hired a couple of successful managers from a successful company, most likely we could have acquired the experience we so desperately needed to run a profitable body shop operation. Walkouts were everyday problems; it was common knowledge that they had one employee in the rest room, one on the way to the rest room, and one on the job. There was no discipline of any kind, the quality was rotten, and it was just one helluva big mess. The body shop lost millions of dollars.

Considering that with the right management it could have been very profitable, someone should have been held *accountable.* The upper echelon was busy adding high-priced officers and drawing large salaries. The war backlog of orders was still creating substantial work. There was no *accountability.* The fact that the fixed-burden rate was much higher than necessary made little difference to big salaries on staff levels.

The DeSoto Engine Plant started about 1951. It was a well-managed operation, compared to the body plant. Certain radical elements tried hard to block progress, but good management kept them under control most of the time. I checked out the engine plant and found they would hire me as a foreman. I took a demotion from the general foreman's job in the metal shop and was transferred to the engine plant as a foreman in the connecting rod department. Three months later, in March 1951, I was promoted to general foreman of the connecting rods, pistons, and camshaft departments. Recognizing that success in these departments depended upon good organization of the human element, I began by working on each operation with each operator. It was easy to find out what the workers liked or disliked about their jobs. I analyzed each worker and came to the conclusion that most wanted to be proud of their work. There was a small percentage that would do as little as possible, yet it was necessary to get an equal workload out of each one. Good supervisors have to be a little bit of everything: psychologist, mechanic, engineer, accountant, and labor relations representative. The best reputation for a supervisor to have is that he is firm but fair.

We also had to get the good will of the maintenance men assigned to us. Sometimes they had it easy when equipment was running well, but they worked their butts off when equipment was down. They were very much interested in quality and productivity. I always made it clear to them how important they were. We appreciated their effort to get us running time.

We also had a good tool trouble man and a good tool engineer assigned to these departments. The response to a trouble call was immediate, and they never left us until we were out of trouble. There are many people who are still living who will remember this, and none will deny that those departments came into line with the best performance and quality anyone could expect. We made a lot of improvements in these departments and accounted for every actual hour used. I was the one held *accountable,* and I carried out my responsibilities. The general superintendent was an excellent manager and a great man to work for but really tight when it came to giving out money.

In 1952 a third son was born, David Michael, making a total of five children. Working as a general foreman and playing the horses now and then, I could not make ends meet, so we gave up our weekends to work in a bar. Martha worked Friday night while I baby-sat. I opened up Saturday morning and helped close up at night, doing the same on Sunday. We put the two older boys to work on paper routes and helping out on milk trucks. As I previously stated, we kept our credit good and had clothes to wear and good food to eat.

From 1952 to 1956 the car requirements had caught up with the backlog, and Chrysler was losing part of the market because our design would not sell. Twice during this period I was passed over for a superintendent's position, and the reason given was that they had no one to replace me with. I took an executive aptitude test in an effort to get into sales; if my grades were high enough, there was an opening for district sales manager. The testing was done by an outside concern. It took three days to take the test, for which the score was read off to me as follows:

Mental ability timed—Average
Mental ability untimed—exceeds 97% of population
Word knowledge—Average
Persuasiveness—Average
Accuracy—Above average
Art—Below average

There were others, but I don't remember them all. The tester's explanation was that I was required to score high in persuasiveness and much better than I had in art; he said that I should do very well in the type of work I was now doing. I did not get the sales job.

In 1956 and 1957 a large burden was added to the staff levels from plant manager on up and several different department heads were also added to plant levels. Consolidation of the plants and restructuring of the staffs were being instituted to improve efficiency to the point where the heavy overhead could be paid for. DeSoto, Dodge, Chrysler and the old six-cylinder Plymouth engines were all transferred to the new Trenton plant. This plant was manufacturing marine and industrial engines and power-steering units. All the big V/8 car and truck engines plus the old flat-head six were going to be built at Trenton.

Whoever was handling the assigning of the personnel necessary to manage this engine plant must have been a rank amateur. The plant manager, the manufacturing manager, and the chief tool engineer were all fine men but definitely not production engine plant men. With four groups of management to pick from, there was no effort made to pick up the best manager or department heads available; instead, the manufacturing manager was a machine-tool salesman. The chief tool engineer was a machine building engineer, and neither knew much about building engines. DeSoto was the first plant to stop making engines. Our general superintendent of production was interviewed for the same position at Trenton. When I talked to him after his interview he told me that there wasn't much chance of his getting the position because he did not know the right people. A few of the DeSoto staff had been transferred to Trenton, but the majority had no idea where they would end up.

In my case the main plant was requesting that I return to the stamp plant and take over the metal-finishing groups again. I went to the operating manager of the main plant and he offered me my old general foreman job back with a small increase in pay. The general foreman of the metal-finishing department on the day shift was retiring, and I was offered the position to replace him. This was in January 1957. The department was using two full shifts plus about forty men on the third shift. It was easy to see that the department had deteriorated badly in the past six years. In my discussion with the operating manager and superintendent of the stamp plant, both agreed that the department was in real trouble— they were running over 100 percent in the red. They were confident I could straighten the department out. I really wanted no part of this setup. I explained to them that my first preference was to be transferred to Trenton. If I refused their offer and then didn't get transferred to Trenton, I would be out of work. Both the operating manager and the general superintendent pointed out to me that if I could get the metal shop producing good performance, they personally would see to it that I would be well compensated for my accomplishments.

After reviewing the department, it was obvious to me that a

27

big improvement wouldn't be a difficult task. I transferred back to the DeSoto main plant and took charge of the metal-finishing department once more.

Two major problems existed: lack of organization and lack of discipline. The quality of the material coming from the stamp plant was extremely poor and required a lot of metal-finishing. The industrial engineering department had two men check with me right away. They wanted to take time studies. I objected, informing them that when I needed them I would send for them, that they knew the conditions today and would be getting reports from me on a daily basis, and that right now all I wanted from them was to chart the program. Anyone who has ever worked as a metal polisher or finisher knows it can't be studied with any degree of accuracy—I had been through that experience years before. To get the best out of the metal shop one had to know the job and then go to work on the human element to get the job done.

I immediately moved in on the bad material from the stamp plant. The stamp plant always liked to run the highest-priced jobs, whether we had a place to store the material or not. One day they were running right-hand front fenders and we had no place to put them. I called the superintendent of the stamp plant and informed him that the department was full, the aisles were full, and that we were damaging the fenders by pitching them ten feet up to land on other piles of sheet metal. His reply was that he didn't give a damn what we did with them, just to get them off the conveyor. Just about ten feet from me a large sheet-metal baler was operating. I thought, that's the only place left to go, so I will just bale all the fenders he runs this afternoon. Then the phone rang and the general foreman of the fender press line informed me that they had pulled their manpower out of the fender lines. If we had baled fenders all afternoon my career with Chrysler would have ended that afternoon.

On the day shift two foremen were working with me, both of whom were capable of doing the work well, but they lacked the aggressiveness to get a fair day's work out of their man-power. My plan of action was to call the supervisor and each employee to my desk to get each employee's reason for his lousy performance. We were using three shifts, but I didn't feel that we even needed two, at least not two full shifts. The industrial engineering department and all my production supervisors agreed with me. When I questioned the workers some gave ridiculous answers; many said they didn't know as no one had told them what the workload was, or said "I ran as many as anyone else." A production figure was given to each man, and it was a figure we knew could be met by anyone doing a fair day's work. In many cases it did exceed the industrial engineering department estimates.

At all times I kept the union steward and committeeman informed of my objectives. My supervisors improved rapidly. We inspired the employees to want to do a better job, we didn't browbeat them, but we didn't hesitate to inform everyone, including the supervisors, that they had a job to do if they intended to stay on the payroll. We meant business and they knew it. I had a reputation for being more than fair, and I expected the same from them.

In thirty days the performance had improved 50 percent. The industrial engineering department and front office were amazed; as soon as we would get an operation meeting their estimate, they would cut the pay for that operation. The efficiency chart showed a steep trend in the right direction. Sixty days later the favorable trend continued. We were banking metal ahead of the paint shop. We laid off part of the third shift. The operating manager and general superintendent congratulated me on the excellent results we were getting. After ninety days that department was beating plan in spite of the price cuts. The rest of the third shift and part of the second shift were laid off. We were finishing more sheet metal with 30 percent fewer men than we had been doing ninety days earlier. The industrial engineering department charts showing the progress were made and copies were distributed. Now was the time to get my promised compensation, my raise in pay.

The general superintendent acknowledged that great progress had been made, but he said he would have to check with his superiors regarding my raise. He evaded me for the next two weeks, and when I caught up with him he had no information. It was easy to see that I was getting the runaround. During February the rest of the engine plant staff had been transferred to Trenton Engine Plant. Many of my friends were trying to get me to come out to the Trenton plant, so I took a trip out there and talked to the general superintendent of manufacturing (Mr. Phillips). He told me that he could use me if I could get released from DeSoto. "I have heard a great deal about you and I think we really need you," he said.

I returned to the DeSoto plant determined to get out. I went to the operating manager and the personnel manager and made my position clear; the personnel manager had a meeting the following day in his office with the operating manager and the president of DeSoto (the general superintendent was on vacation). All were unanimous in their opinion of my progress and the improvement of the metal shop, and they asked if I would stay if they raised my pay. My answer was no; I had come back to this plant on condition that when the job was completed I would be compensated, but I had failed to receive the compensation. "You all agree that I have an excellent record of accomplishments," I said. "Now all I ask of you is a transfer to the Trenton engine plant with a favorable recommendation."

They made the decision to allow me to accept the position at Trenton. It was June 1, 1957, and they asked me to wait until September before transferring.

I replied, "How in hell long do you think they will keep that job open for me at Trenton? I will train a man to take my place in the metal shop. The transfer must be much sooner. You want me to wait until September, but we can split the difference and you can transfer me by the fifteenth of July."

They agreed and I was transferred to the Trenton Engine plant on July 15. I would be on special assignment, reporting to the general superintendent of manufacturing. My first observations of the plant were that it was full of opportunities. It was a large manufacturing facility full of equipment that was supposed to build parts for and assemble engines economically. The college boys really had this plant loaded with new concepts, but it was easy to see that whoever was supposed to be *accountable* for tooling this installation had very little experience in production machining.

Chapter 11

My first assignment was on the V/8 connecting rods. The major problems centered around badly designed fixtures and forgings that were out of specifications. The fixtures and clamping had to be revised on the Natco wrist-pin hole drilling machine and on the Buhr bolt-hole drilling machine. The bottom chamfer tools on the wrist pin hole were breaking as fast as you could set them up and install them. Likewise, the spot facing tools on the cap nut seat were breaking as fast as they could be installed. We threw out the bottom chamfer tools and installed a single spindle drill press. We eliminated the problem on the spot facing by getting rid of the drill presses and installing a broach. I would estimate we lost a half million before the corrective action was taken.

Two lines were running side by side; one was low volume, which we called the raised "B" line, the other was high volume, which we called the low "B" line. Some of the equipment was interchangeable. The capacity of the two lines was supposed to be about 8,000 O.K. rods per shift, but we were producing somewhere around 3,500. The weight mills would not hold weight; we kept the vendor busy for several weeks getting weight under control.

We were adding to the problem by sending rods into the mills that were outside the correction range. The Trio assembly machines were continuously down. We disposed of them and went to bench assembly with torque guns and presses. The boring of the pin and crank bores was done with new machines which were scrap generators. The finish internal grinders had more mechanics working on them than operators. What a field day the salesmen must have had when tooling this plant! Believe me, the stockholders took an unbelievable loss, one that ran into millions of dollars. It was inconceivable that a company in business as long as Chrysler could tool a plant so badly for high-volume production. With this kind of management it was easy to see why we made a lot of other companies rich while we struggled to break even.

The next assignment was the piston department. The DeSoto piston line at the Warren plant would produce 3,200 pistons per shift with eleven employees (no automation). The Trenton piston line was a triple setup completely automated: the raised "B" line was a single line, the low "B" was a double line. The roll count for the department was eighty-seven men and women. They were producing 3,500 to 4,000 per shift. On the low "B" line there were eight Cincinnati skirt O.D. grinders. The automation hadn't been hooked up; the foreman had two men on each machine loading and unloading. My first move was to eliminate eight men out of this group, because one man could easily load and unload each machine. Because it was jamming and damaging pistons we had to throw out the whole conveyor system. We installed steel belt conveyors. I can't even begin to estimate the cost of this conversion. The excess number of employees and the scrap and repairs again ran into millions of dollars of stockholders' money. Somebody in the top echelon should have been *accountable*, but who? It was considered a launching operation and no one seemed to be excited about the cost.

Another department that cost millions of dollars (and much of it had to be replaced later) was the V/8 crankshaft line. The

Sundstrand lathes and their automation, plus the walking beam automation and the Wilson automation, eventually all had to be disposed of and replaced with other types of equipment. During this time the production was about 30 percent of capacity. In spite of a concentrated effort to correct the problems, until we replaced the equipment we were fighting a losing battle. *Accountability?* There wasn't any! Some men who held high positions then are *still* holding them.

In the fall of 1957 I was appointed production coordinator for the plant. I still reported to the general superintendent of production. My duties consisted of setting up variance and efficency reporting systems throughout the plant. I also worked with the industrial engineering and budget departments and made the advance production forecasting. The forecasting was revised monthly. Today a large number of people get involved in that, all the way up to the V.P.; there isn't much improvement over the days when I did it except it costs a lot more now. We were building the marine and industrial engines, and stands and sirens. Stands were engines enclosed in a stationary position. These were used to drive cement mixers and irrigation pumps, and to provide power for a large number of other types of equipment. Each required a special buildup. We had a short V/8 industrial engine buildup line and a short six-cylinder industrial engine buildup line. We also had a marine engine building and testing area. The industrial engines were all painted red except army engines, which were painted drab. Marine and industrial engines were scattered throughout the plant, most in some state of repair. There must have been a thousand different models. The docks were loaded with partial orders that couldn't be shipped without getting the rest of the engines to make a complete order. On January 1, 1958, I was put in charge of all activities regarding marine and industrial engine building and shipping. The manufacturing manager was replaced and we got a new manager. After a couple of weeks he instructed me to write him a communication on just how I planned to get the M & I (marine and industrial) engine operation into a smooth-running unit. I wrote the communication and after a week reported to his office. He had reviewed my plans, approved of them, and he told me that as of now I would report directly to him. He wanted a crash program undertaken to clear the plant of all engines that were scattered throughout in various states of repair and to build the engines necessary to fill the orders on the dock and ship them.

My plan of operating the M & I engine program worked to perfection: we never started an engine we couldn't build and immediately rebuilt any engine that failed to get to the shipping dock for any reason. We mixed our housing jobs and our transmission jobs with the more simple buildups so that we could get the maximum number OKd per day. We programmed our dress-up lines, both V/8 and six-cylinder, so that when we changed the mix we also changed line speed. We brought productivity from twenty-five engines per day to 120 engines per day, without adding a man. It was just a simple matter of organization, getting a damn good group of men to put their talent to work.

In the summer of 1958 a decision was made to make more room at Trenton for domestic passenger car and truck engines. The M & I operation would be moved to the Jefferson plant. The move was started immediately and completed in the early fall. A manager was selected to run this operation at the Jefferson plant. He asked me to go with him as production manager. I accepted, but when the manufacturing manager heard I was planning on going with the M & I operation, he called me into his office and asked why.

"It was a better job with more money," I answered.

His reply to that was, "Well, you're not going. You will be promoted to superintendent of the steel division on Monday. You mean too much to this plant to let you go with M & I."

Chapter 12

The first of October, 1958, I took charge of the steel and aluminum division, consisting of V/8 rockershafts, V/8 cranks, V/8 rods, V/8 pistons, six-cylinder aluminum and cast-iron piston and water and oil pumps. The salary was $750 per month. Two general foremen on my staff were former superintendents, whose salaries were $850 per month. To catch up with them and pass them I would have to be *accountable.* My responsibilities were to direct all phases of this division to a successful performance. Since planning and organization were my strong suit, it would be just a matter of time.

My time in the plant usually ran ten hours per day, but without overtime pay, and sometimes included Saturday and Sunday, with no compensation. Many times I wished that when my day was over I could leave the plant and all its problems and go home and forget for a while, but this was impossible for me. I solved many problems at night when I should have been sleeping. I never used an alarm clock—never needed one.

The steel division was improving daily—we were making progress. Our manufacturing manager was promoted to plant manager and we got a new manufacturing manager. He was young and rough, a tool engineer by trade. He used little diplomacy and plenty of foul language. I think of him when I use the term "browbeating" leadership. He really wasn't too bad if you stood up to him, especially if your division was running well.

The steel division was running fairly well, comparatively speaking, but the V/8 block and head division were in trouble, so in early 1959 the orders were that I would exchange positions with the block division superintendent. The blocks and heads were new to me—I was to concentrate on V/8 blocks. My first day was eighteen hours long, and I went home and drew a layout of the block department. Then each day I added to that layout, putting in the equipment—what machining was done on the block and what the capacity was. The tool change and gauging frequencies were also a part of my notes. After a couple of weeks I started to plan and organize the supervisors and employees. We all had to be working with the same objectives in mind.

Our plant manager and engineering department were in the midst of launching the slant six-cylinder engines. They had a timetable to meet; fortunately, the plant manager was a man of action who knew what he was doing—he would meet his schedule. A new supervisory group would have to be selected to man the new departments. The superintendent of steel was given this assignment; as a result, the steel division was returned to me but I still retained the cast-iron division. This gave me two offices, two clerks and two-thirds of all the machining in the plant. I received a good increase in salary.

Our fourth son, Ronald James, was born in February 1960. On this same date our oldest son was inducted into the armed services. We now had four sons and two daughters. I remarked at the staff meeting that the employment department was having a hard time filling manpower requisitions, but that I had lost a son to the Army and had received a replacement the same day.

After about three months the plant manager called me to his office and told me he was hiring two new superintendents, one for the cast-iron division and one for the steel division. I was going to the second shift as plant shift superintendent. I objected—I wanted no part of the second shift. The new superintendents were outsiders—why should they get the day shift positions? But he would not listen to me.

"I am training you for something better, so just make a good showing on the second shift and keep your feet on the floor," he said.

I went on the second shift sometime around July 1, 1960. The manufacturing manager, having been promoted to a new position in South America, was replaced with another (the fourth since I came to Trenton). The new one was a quality control man who knew very little about building engines. In the fall the plant manager gave up his position and was replaced by the plant manager who was at Trenton when I first came there. The plant performance was terrible. The new manufacturing manager wanted my opinion as to what was wrong. I advised him that the two new superintendents were meeting a great deal of resistance and were making no progress. I felt that supervisory changes were necessary. He listened and then said, "I want you to know how I operate. As plant shift superintendent on the second shift you are the second shift plant manager."

I asked him if he were planning on reorganizing the supervisory staff and he replied, "Definitely, and as soon as possible."

"Well," I said, "the plant manager position on the second shift is open. I would rather be a small cog on the first shift than a big wheel on the second shift."

"OK," he said. "What area do you want?"

"The steel division."

"If I give you the steel division, you also have to take the six-cylinder rods, miscellaneous machining, and the six- and eight-cylinder camshafts. This would involve about 700 employees."

I wanted my regular clerk back, as she could handle a large area. He agreed and told me to report to the first shift on the following Monday morning. The date was September 1960.

Chapter 13

During this period our upper echelon had acquired the services of a new controller. He had been with an accounting firm and joined us in 1957. In 1958 he was named group vice president of international operations, in 1960 an administrative vice president, and president in 1961. In four years he had gone from controller to president of a multi-billion-dollar automobile company. In 1959 we acquired the services of another accountant, who joined us as a staff executive on the international operations staff. In 1960 he became the general manager of the important-export division. In 1961 he was elected vice president of Chrysler Canada Ltd. Two years from accountant to vice president. As stated in the proxy statement, he held many high positions and eventually became president of the same multi-billion-dollar automobile company. The total unit sales in 1960 were 1,183,311. The total sales in 1961 were 802,003, a drop of over 350,000 units. Our percentage of the 1960 market in total cars, trucks and buses was 13.8 percent; in 1961 it was 10.9 percent. In 1962 we built 892,299 units, an increase in units but a drop in market penetration to 9.9 percent.

Our new president took immediate and drastic action. He was accurately aware that in order to make a profit we had to make cars that would sell, and even more important had to make more money than was spent. He ordered an austerity program to go into effect throughout the corporation. Cost-cutting across the board was our only salvation. He also hired a new designer whose methods were extremely effective.

In 1963 our market penetration climbed back to 12.7 percent. 1,518,586 units were built. In 1964 market penetration was 14.8 percent. 1,807,258 units were built.

At this time we were starting to make money, and at this time we also acquired another high-priced salesman who was later to become president. We were electing vice presidents and appointing large staffs like they were going out of style. All of these statements are borne out if you read the prospectus dated April 23, 1965, and the proxy dated April 16, 1968.

In the latter part of 1960 or early 1961 our manufacturing manager was promoted. A new one was appointed who was a tool engineer and was very helpful. He made several improvements in several departments. In 1961 another plant manager was assigned to Trenton. He was an excellent manager and an aggressive action man. Trenton Engine progressed under his direction—he was a good mechanic and a good administrator. He added the V/8 head lines to my group. They were running about 200 percent off standard. Using the same methods and type of leadership that had been so successful in the past, I personally discussed the V/8 head department with each operator, job setter, supervisor, maintenance supervisor, and tool engineer, and held a meeting every four hours to review our progress or obstacles. Operators and job setters became interested in producing cylinder heads. The department was soon running at a reasonable performance level.

Our good manufacturing manager was promoted and we were assigned another manufacturing manager. He was an academic genius but had no practical experience and he shook up the whole plant. His dissatisfaction with the production and maintenance staffs resulted in a number of demotions and supervisory changes. I was moved from my position to the six-cylinder steel division, which included six-cylinder rods, cranks, heads, and manifolds. These departments were controlling the output of the assembly line. Our six-cylinder requirements were 2,800 engines per day. We were building two types of six-cylinder engines, the small 170-cubic-inch and the large 225-cubic-inch. The machining departments were running seven days per week. Operators were performing at about 65 percent of capacity. Many new drill heads had to be bought for the head lines. The crank line was running fairly well, but the rest of the departments needed and received a quick reorganization. I worked around the clock to break operator resistance. As always, 90 percent wanted to do what was right while 10 percent tried to control productivity.

It took about six months to get this department on plan. I received a 10 percent merit increase in pay. When I thanked the plant manager he remarked, "You do your job and I'll do mine." I also received a $4,100 bonus that year. You can be sure I was very pleased.

The latest manufacturing manager quit. Another one was assigned to us and he made some organizational changes. I was assigned to be superintendent of all V/8 cranks, rods, six-cylinder cranks, and six-cylinder rods. This had some advantages, as supervisors and operators were interchangeable.

Our plant manager was moved to the Jefferson plant and we received another plant manager. He was not what you would call a mechanic or engine man; however, he had managed machining plants. He was an excellent administrator, an inspirational leader. I know of no one who did not try to do his best for this man. In 1965 the manufacturing manager was promoted and another was assigned to us. This made seven manufacturing managers and four plant managers in eight years.

I was close to the top of my grade and I felt ready for the general superintendent's position. I was interviewed for the job of manufacturing manager of the Windsor engine plant, but I wanted more money than they were willing to pay and did not get the job.

About six months later my boss, the general superintendent, was promoted to a new position, which opened up an opportunity for me. I was promoted to fill this position. I can still remember the plant manager's little speech when he announced my appointment to his staff. All the department heads were in the executive conference room when I walked in with the manufacturing manager and the general superintendent.

The plant manager stood up and said, "You were all aware that Bob was being transferred to a new assignment. We have selected Ed Gallaway as our general superintendent of manufacturing. We are not giving this job to Ed because he has brown eyes and black hair. Ed has earned this position. You all know that in these days of degrees, Ed would have to be head and shoulders over anyone else to have gotten this position."

Everyone congratulated me. I was proud—now I would have to justify their confidence in me.

The high echelon of the corporation continued to add degrees to the already overloaded staffs. In 1965 a new general plants manager was appointed. He was an expert on plant cleanliness and also did a lot of talking about job enrichment, but to my knowledge the only job he was ever able to enrich successfully was his own. He even got a boost in pay while we were losing $52 million. Throughout this book I have proven that millions of dollars were made for the company by men with common sense but without degrees, yet from a grade thirteen up there was very little chance of getting a position without a degree. I could consider myself lucky to have gotten a grade thirteen, even though I had made the company millions of dollars. Graduation from the college of hard knocks would not be recognized. I have always felt that everyone should get as much education as possible, but many men with degrees are vastly overrated. When you are working as general superintendent of manufacturing, a degree doesn't mean much. Good results are the determining factor in whether you can handle the position or not. The stockholders know what the price of stock is and also when and how much the dividend is. With good top management stocks don't drop 75 percent in two years and dividends don't disappear.

About August 1968 our plant manager was promoted to general plants manager, so a new plant manager was assigned to Trenton Engine. This was his first chance as a plant manager. At first, in my opinion, he listened too much to the comptroller, the industrial engineer, and the personnel manager, none of whom could have run the simplest line in any production department, so we did not get off to a very good start. Also, I was due for a merit increase and he held that up for some time. He had a habit of listening to many people who misled him; other than that I thought he had a lot of good points. He was aggressive, ambitious, and was a hard worker. After spending a great deal of time out in the plant he realized how much he was being misled by his front office group—he came face to face with reality. He and I worked pretty close together from that point on.

Volume was down in 1970-71, so there was no incentive compensation for those two years. We changed manufacturing managers in the fall of 1969. Assigned to us was a college-degree man with high hopes of getting to the top fast. He was years younger than I and had moved very rapidly up to this point. His type of leadership and mine clashed—I was not mean enough to suit him. He was very much misled by one particular individual, but he was exceptionally quick to learn the important parts of his responsibilities. He told me he wouldn't be easy, and he lived up to his word. He was a hard worker, good on follow-up, and a tough man to satisfy in regard to good housekeeping, quality, scrap control, and repairs. He was continuously prodding. Many things were not as easy to do as he made them sound, but I felt he was doing his job and he was good for the plant.

Chapter 14

Before I complete my part of the action from 1970 to 1975, I think it is time to say that up to this point I have reported only on my own activities and the many changes in plant management as they occurred. I have repeatedly said that on each assignment I was held *accountable*. The stockholders had every right to expect this. My reason for early retirement was to write this book, hoping to attract the attention of the shareholders and employees and to alert them to the seriousness of our position. Holding everyone *accountable* from the chairman of the board to the hourly employee can turn this corporation around. We can compete with General Motors and Ford, which we haven't done for a long time. I didn't feel that I could stay on the active payroll and write this book without expecting the higher officers to terminate my employment. I am by no stretch of the imagination wealthy. I have about 1,700 shares of stock; you shareholders know what that is worth compared to what it should be worth with good management. The dividends that retirees depend on have been eliminated. *Accountability* by every department head from vice president on down would save millions of dollars. Why do we need so many vice presidents? Shareholders have the power to bring that number down to what is actually required. There are too many men on the upper staff who have been nothing but a burden for some time.

We all agree that "Chrysler Builds Great Cars," Chrysler has great engineering, the styling is beautiful, and in many ways we have more talent than our competitors; but we also have much more deadwood. Can anyone imagine over $11 billion in sales and a loss of $52 million? At the stockholders' meeting, the officers tried to defend their bad management by blaming the difficult times, the high cost of material and labor, and last but not least, the cost of government-mandated control. To my knowledge, Ford and General Motors operate here in this same United States, so their problems must have been the same. While their profits were down, they still made a profit, and while they cut their dividends, they still paid a dividend. After reviewing the proxy with regard to our board of directors, it is apparent that all have been very successful and are well educated men and women. Most are wealthy, perhaps all—the board is loaded with bankers, accountants, and lawyers; but when $11 billion in sales results in $52 million in loss, we shareholders better start changing the board so that $11 billion in sales will result in five or six cents profit on the dollar. The 1974 annual report to shareholders states that our market penetration of the domestic small-car market was nearly 24 percent. Valiant set new sales records, outselling all of the small compact cars. In 1974, combined sales of Valiant and Dart models captured nearly 40 percent of the domestic compact market. Can we forget that even with all of this favorability, our competition made a profit and paid good dividends, while we lost $52 million and paid no first-quarter dividend? Another interesting item for us shareholders to look at is in the annual report regarding major appointments. In June 1974, six new vice presidents were elected; in July two more were elected, in September one more, in October two more, in November one more, and in December one group vice president was elected executive vice president. All of these promotions, you can be sure, cost the shareholders a large sum of money for fat increases in salaries. All of this happened while we were losing $52 million from sales of $11 billion. We were supposed to be cutting costs, not creating plush, high-salaried positions. This same group has access to shareholder-owned jet airplanes that they fly all over the world at shareholders' expense, with an open expense account.

At the stockholders' meeting the chairman stated that no incentive compensation had been paid for 1974. In the opening chapter there was some comment on the incentive compensation plan. I have stated previously that in 1964 I received a bonus of $4,100; at that time incentive compensation was paid to all executives from grade nine on up, but in 1970 or 1971 the incentive compensation rules were changed. Grades nine, ten, and eleven were eliminated from the bonus roll—these grades were paid by getting cost-of-living allowances and overtime. Many of them resented being eliminated from the bonus roll. In 1971 many of us were working seven days a week; it turned out that grades nine, ten, and eleven made out very well because they were paid overtime. I was a grade thirteen, and all my ten-hour days, Saturdays, and Sundays were worked for no compensation. The following year, 1972, there were only about 1,400 bonus-roll executives; the elimination of grades nine, ten, and eleven had reduced eligible executives from about 4,400 to 1,400. In comparing my bonus with a like position at General Motors and Ford there was a big difference. Now, I thought with a much smaller bonus roll I was bound to get a decent bonus, but this was not the case. The incentive compensation committee gave most of the money to the top officers, and very little dribbled down to plant-level executives, where all the money had to originate and where most of the hard work had to be done, with executives such as myself working ten hours a day and five to six hours each Saturday and Sunday. As general superintendent, grade thirteen, I received a bonus of $6,000— remember, I got no cost-of-living or overtime pay. The compensation for about 800 hours of premium time was about $7.50 per hour. I was extremely disappointed and hoped the incentive compensation committee would do a better job of distribution the following year of 1973. In 1973 the money set aside for compensation was about $19 million (it had been a good year for Chrysler), but the plant executives again received the short end of the stick. My extra hours amounted to 950, but my bonus was exactly the same, $6,000. Most of the money had gone to the top officers again, the same officers who find excuses for the $52 million loss, the loss of dividends, and the discontinuance of the stock plan, but are unable to find failures in their methods of management.

The incentive compensation committee, as stated in the proxy statement on page 14, granted stock options of 574,500 shares at $12.72 per share to fifty-five directors and officers as a group. 190,000 shares went to the top four officers on page 10 of the proxy. In addition to their excessive salaries, the directors and officers as a group received $159,767 worth of stock from the thrift-stock program—contributions that have to be earned according to the plan. I do not know of any options or free stock to anyone at plant-manager or lower than plant-manager executive level. There is absolutely no justi- fication for this type of distribution. I note that four of the largest vendors are on the incentive compensation committee. The same committee handles the retirement plan. I retired after thirty-eight and a half years; page 12 of the proxy shows that once you reach twenty-five years of service and average $30,000 for five years there is no incentive to work any longer: the pension equals 50 percent of your pay after twenty-five years of service, and yet still equals only 50 percent after thirty-five years at age sixty-five. Where is the justice in this program for me, who started at eighteen? Who can change all this? The annual report shows there are 232,435 shareholders. At this point, with the stock at ten dollars and no dividends, there should be 200,000 dissatisfied shareholders—they control this corporation. They can replace every director or officer if they so desire. There are many very capable men and women in Chrysler corporation, but they can't move while the present board and officers are still in charge. The 32,435 shareholders that I did not mention as dissatisfied were the officers, plus all the vice presidents and their huge staffs, who would not dare vote against the proxy for fear of losing their jobs. From my point of view we shareholders can sit still and do nothing (in which case we may have a very uncertain future with regard to stock prices and dividends) or we can get organized and turn this great corporation around to become competitive with Ford and General Motors. We have very little to lose and a great deal to gain.

———————*Chapter 15*———————

Fellow shareholders, did you vote your shares or did you just ignore the proxy and take the position, "Oh, what's the use, there's nothing I can do. The board of directors and officers are too big and too powerful for me to fight. I'll just sit back and hope for the best?" I am sure millions of shares were not voted because of this type of attitude on the part of many shareholders. Remember, nothing happens by itself, someone has to make it happen. Shareholders own this corporation and there is nothing they cannot do if they get organized and make the changes that are necessary. Don't take the position that "it hasn't been done before, so why would anyone think it can be done now?" Many things in this world happen because someone makes them happen. For the love of a woman the king of England gave up his throne—who ever thought that would happen? A call girl upset the English Parliament—amazing, isn't it, what can be done when someone makes something happen? What more do we need to entice us to get into action? $11 billion in sales and $52 million in losses; no thrift-stock plan; no dividends; cuts in pay, because cost-of-living allowances for most salaried workers were eliminated; cuts in pay for bonus executives, including executives who received such a low bonus that subordinates outdrew them with overtime pay and cost-of-living allowance. What more incentive do we need to motivate us into taking some corrective action? Are we going to give up and concede that we can't compete with our competitors? I am sure we have much more determination and pride than this.

However, if you need more incentive, let me refer you to page 27 of the 1974 Chrysler Corporation annual report. Read carefully the item on common stock. Note that of the 80 million authorized shares as of December 30, 1974, 1,483,950 shares were reserved for stock option for salaried officers and key employees under the qualified and non-qualified stock option plan. Options for 420,500 shares were granted at $8.82 per share on January 16, 1975. All options were granted at prices not less than 100 percent of market value at dates of grant. Do you fellow shareholders believe that with good management stock would have dropped to this level? Fellow shareholders, to my knowledge none of these options ever gets down to plant level, where the actual work has to be done and where the profits have to be made. Incentive should be created where the profits have to be made.

The corporation puts out an excellent proxy statement and annual report—if you read it you will know everything except where all the money went; it also explains in some detail how great all our products are. With these facts being true, how can any shareholder accept the explanation for our $52 million loss, while the competition made a profit and paid a good dividend? The difference has to be in how the corporation was managed. On page 6 of the annual report is a statement to the effect that shortages of steel, castings, petrochemicals, and other commodities are expected to persist in the automobile industry throughout the end of the decade. However, it is generally agreed that sales will return to more normal levels and will continue into the 1980's and beyond. What more sales do we need? Eleven billion dollars in sales resulted in $52 million loss. Do not the same shortages prevail for our competitors? They expect to make profits and pay dividends in this decade. Fellow shareholders and employees, do any of you expect a dividend or big increase in our stock price in the near future? Let us review pages 18 and 19 of the annual report and the 1975 proxy statement reports that salaries and fees for all fifty-five directors and officers as a group were $3,602,528 in 1974. Subtract fifteen of the board of directors who drew salaries of only $10,000. That leaves forty-one officers and key executives to share $3,452,528 and this doesn't include stock options or corporation thrift-stock contribution! Really, fellow shareholders, this is quite a burden; just imagine what the total is when you add all their staffs, and they all have more than adequate staffs. How many automobiles do you think we have to build and sell just to pay the salaries of the organization shown on pages 18 and 19 of the annual report? Each has to have a large staff to justify his existence. We shareholders should make each one *accountable*: what does each staff cost and of what value in actual dollars has it been to the corporation? In my opinion, the $52 million loss could have been eliminated just in a reasonable reduction of this staff. I am sure there are a number of good men on this staff; we should keep the best and release the rest to get the burden down somewhere near where it must be to operate at a profit.

Fellow shareholders, when this corporation started going in the right direction in the early sixties, the new designer we hired from one of our competitors was a real shot in the arm.

It will always be considered one of the best moves the board chairman ever made. We were in desperate need then and are still in desperate need of a foundry expert. Any one of our tool engineers would attest to the fact that we can't compete with our competitors with regard to castings. This isn't any new thing—our machine shops are in continuous trouble because of bad castings and forgings. It also costs more to produce these castings in our plants than it costs to purchase them from our competitors. At Trenton Engine we are paying twenty-two dollars more per six-cylinder head from our own foundry than we could get a good head for from an outside vendor. Cast crankshafts were eight dollars less per crank by purchasing good cranks from an outside vendor. Shareholders, are you beginning to realize why we lost $52 million in 1974? Where is the *accountability* that we have every right to expect from the forge and foundry divisions?

Our international operations may be necessary to expand our corporation, but I see only one annual report where, excluding Canada, we made any profits. Where is the *accountability* of the international operations? Shareholders should know which countries are profitable and which ones are costing us money. We should insist on getting out of those without profits. How long is it going to take us before someone is put in charge of our international operations who can compete with our competitors? More than 100,000 foreign-made cars have been sold per month in the United States this year. Our sales department should interview many of these buyers. Perhaps we could find out what is so appealing about those cars, but of course if our sales department takes the position that nothing can be done about it, maybe by the end of the year sales can get up to 200,000 per month. You can be sure grass won't grow under their feet.

The *Detroit News* has an article on the front page in large print: "More Chrysler Rebates on the Way." Fellow shareholders, the great tragedy of this is that many of our cars sold at discount and rebate prices were built on premium time.

Many of the machining departments were working Saturday and Sunday while this large bank of automobiles was built and parked in fields. Planning *accountability*? There wasn't any. We also had a large number of 1974 models to sell. What action has been taken with regard to the executives who caused many of the problems that cost this corporation millions of dollars? Since they are not *accountable*, why aren't they relieved of their positions? If there has been any action taken, the shareholders have a right to know what the action was.

Chapter 16

In our annual report, pages 18 and 19, the organizational chart indicates that we have two vice-presidents in charge of purchasing. Purchasing material, equipment, tools, and services can make or break a corporation. When we make appointments, the vice presidents on down through the purchasing agents to the tool store supervisors should be well-qualified personnel. The proxy statement, page 9, states that in 1974 the corporation and its subsidiaries in the ordinary course of business purchased materials, supplies, and services from over 2,500 nationally known concerns, and total purchases amounted to approximately $7 billion. Included among the purchases were the following: from B. A. S. F. Wyandotte Corporation, chemicals aggregating $2,500,000 (the chairman of the corporation is on our board of directors and is a member of the incentive compensation committee); from the Burroughs Corporation, data-processing equipment purchased or leased for amounts aggregating $930,000 under contracts which terminate in 1977 and 1979 and require lease payments of $2,701,100 per year (the chairman of the Burroughs Corporation is one of our board of directors and a member of our incentive compensation committee); from Hewlett-Packard company we purchased electronic equipment, an aggregate of $275,000 (the president is on our board of directors and is a member of our incentive compensation committee). In 1974 Chrysler Corporation paid to the law firm of Kelley, Dyre, Warren, fees of $668,929 for services as counselor for the corporation (a member of this firm is on our board of directors and is also a member of our incentive compensation committee). A news article in the *Detroit News* on March 27, 1975, states that Burroughs' net profit for the full year of 1974 rose 23 percent to 143 million or $3.66 per share; sales rose 19 percent to 1.53 billion; both were all-time highs. These results show what can be done with good management.

Fellow shareholders, when we are spending $7 billion we must have men of the highest caliber as purchasing agents, especially trained to get the most for our money. We have a chemical plant, an electrical plant, and a law firm. Are we getting the full benefits from our own plants and firms? Accountability should be shown that would eliminate the possibility that much of our 1974 loss was not caused by inexperience in the purchasing department. In the annual report, page 14, major appointments were made or new positions were created to the extent that the average stock-holder would think the corporation had plenty of money, when in reality each increase in cost helped add to the $52 million cash loss, plus all the other losses suffered by the lower supervisory group, including plant-level bonus executives. A new vice president of purchasing was elected; what were his qualifications to become the head of purchasing? The proxy, as I have pointed out, lists this as a $7 billion operation. I think the shareholders have a right to know what his previous position was. As a general plants manager, what were his accomplishments? If the group he headed ever made its profit plan, it was never on any reports that I had access to. Our foundry problems could never be considered anything but the worst. His staff of purchasing agents can be the difference between making or losing millions of dollars. Our follow-up men and tool-stores men do not get paid the necessary wage to make them the best men possible to handle millions of dollars. With a major rehabilitation and expansion program just completed at Trenton Engine, where much of the equipment has yet to be installed, there's a lot more debugging to do on today's equipment than on that used in all my years with the corporation. We have to rebuild some of the new equipment to make it run. Purchasing should be held *accountable* for what it purchased. No equipment should be paid for until all specifications are met, and the department should be involved in shortages and inferior tools. It should be *accountable* for all the production losses because of tool and equipment shortages; it should be *accountable* for all the tools and equipment parts that we have to pay double- and triple-time for and have delivered by taxicab. Seven billion dollars is a great deal of money. We can't put too much emphasis on getting our money's worth.

The corporate planning of the production scheduling has been very ineffective. This group must accept responsibilities for building, on premium time, cars and trucks that later had to be sold at a discount. They have a million reasons for the millions of dollars their poor planning cost the corporation. When an engine plant has to change assembly line speeds and machine shop schedules every three or four weeks, with the labor contracts we have today it causes a vast shuffle of manpower; this reduces output, creates excessive training, increases scrap and repair, and hurts quality. Anyone in the top echelon who believes a body is a body and all you have to do is move it around does not belong in the planning and scheduling department. Every schedule change costs hundreds of thousands of dollars. We had to change schedules so often that we became quite efficient at it. However, it still cost a lot of money; it also kept the labor force in a very unstable state of mind. The *accountability* of the planning and scheduling departments was completely unsatisfactory to this shareholder and would be to millions of others if the facts were known.

Corporate engineering has the reputation of achieving many firsts in its efforts to stay ahead of the rest of the industry. However, the department must be held *accountable* for the excessive mix which causes many problems on the assembly lines and does nothing to simplify operations on the assembly lines. Our financial position forces us to make many changes now that could have been made much sooner. It seems that we have to get desperate to get maximum effort out of our corporate staffs. Refer to page 5 of the annual report; the report states that in response to the rapid deterioration of the world economy, the company intensifies its efforts to improve sales and to reduce fixed costs and expense in all areas of its operations. As sales fell off we cut back on production schedules and curtailed many of our staff operations; we intensified our program of streamlining our worldwide operations by combining similiar operations and simplifying through product standardization. It would appear we always lock the barn after the horse is gone. Many of our top engineers never got close enough to the assembly operation. They should get out of the lab and visit the plant once in a while, in spite of what has just been reported on page 5 of the annual report. Why did we build so many '75 models with such a large backlog of '74 models built and not sold? In our streamlining of the operations, how many of the vice president operations were combined and how many did we reduce to lower positions?

Up to this point I have been very critical of the corporate officers and have outlined my reasoning.

Chapter 17

We used to have one vice president who handled labor relations and personnel; now we have two, and when contracts are negotiated we have a large number of experts from the personnel, labor relations, budget, industrial engineering, and legal staffs, but no one from the departments where most of the problems originate. The jobs aren't all the same out in the plant where the money has to be made. Some of the concessions made by our negotiating committee must have come from some book they read while they were in college, and of course they expect all the lesser-educated production personnel to put all of the concessions into effect. It would be wise to add a couple of good production superintendents to the negotiating team, then maybe there would be someone who understood the language of the stewards, committeemen, and officers of the union who are elected by the employees of the plant to negotiate for them. Our personnel and labor relations representatives make many concessions for fear of a walkout. Executives in the plants who are out on the floor where the money has to be made are much more familiar with the working conditions, plus the causes, and would be of great benefit to the bargaining team. Of course, many of them have only practical experience, not college degrees. The union uses working conditions as the main threat in gaining their objectives. They accept no responsibility for bad working conditions their members create for themselves. It must be remembered that good work conditions start with the construction of the plant, where working conditions and housekeeping were not a consideration. Most of our plants were built before these items became big issues.

Our brilliant representatives, most of whom will never work inside of a manufacturing area, grant all types of concessions that are detrimental to good housekeeping and working conditions. Coffee machines, candy machines, and soft-drink machines are scattered throughout the plant. The right to drink or eat at any time the workers please and as many times as they wish creates bad working conditions and garbage throughout the plant, since very few employees ever get in the habit of using the garbage barrels provided for their use. Most of our competitors restrict the areas where employees must remain while eating or drinking—this reduces the number of janitors needed and helps a great deal in keeping the plant clean.

Water and oil on the floor will always be a problem in plants. These items were not considered when equipment installations were made; of course there is no excuse for stock on the floor, disorderly stock arrangement, or miscellaneous items lying all over the place. Representatives of the bargaining team should spend six months out in some of the manufacturing departments and have the responsibility of keeping working conditions and housekeeping in satisfactory condition; then they might recognize the task involved. Every time we expected a visit from one of the top officers we spent a minimum of $20,000 to dress up the plant. I believe in respecting my superiors, but in return they should earn that respect. These people should realize that the wealth of the corporation is created in the production plants, not in the staff office at Highland Park. The union was able to negotiate an annual wage improvement into the contract; the only guarantee was that it would be paid—no conditions were set forth as to how it was going to be generated. Chrysler concept was that it would be generated through cost-reduction programs. The union wasn't a party to any of these. The truth is we never recovered the annual improvement costs, regardless of the phony figures that our industrial engineering departments come up with.

The union officials representing the workers did a commendable job of getting all types of benefits for their membership. Most of the benefits the union won for their membership were passed on to most salaried employees up through the lower executive level. Naturally, the salaried employees were always hopeful that the union would win big concessions—what other way would they be properly compensated, unless the union won it for them? Anyone with common sense knows the only way to recover these excessive costs would be to pass them on to the consumer. When our top officers say the increased costs haven't been recovered, it only means we gave away too much. How much intelligence does anyone need to know you can't manufacture anything at a loss and still stay in business? The union should teach its membership that to drain the company of all resources only jeopardizes their own security. You can't get blood out of a stone; also, buying other makes or foreign products doesn't improve their job status, or show that they have any pride in their own workmanship. My opinion is: in addition to getting all the improved working conditions they can get, they also have the responsibility to help keep the company that's going to pay all these benefits in a strong competitive position or risk the complete loss of everything they have gained. Incompetence by both company and union will surely result in going out of business.

Another expense handled by personnel was recruiting college graduates and bringing them into our plants as management trainees. Most of these special-privilege individuals work out fine on the upper staffs or front office jobs, where there is no *accountability* and very little to do. It was a different story when they were assigned out in the plant as production foremen; after a month's training 95 percent of them made it clear that this was not their idea of a good way to earn a living. Their education entitled them to easier ways and they intended to stay in the front-office jobs. I know of no personnel-selected management trainee who was ever successful at the Trenton Engine Plant. Why are we wasting money on this type of project? A news item reports that the Bureau of Labor Statistics estimates that the number of college graduates will exceed the number of jobs requiring their skills by 800,000 between now and 1985, that the glut of college grads will reach a peak between 1980 and 1985, at which time there will be 140,000 over-trained college graduates each year. The Gallup poll reports, in large print, "College students mistrust business, only twenty percent of the college students interviewed believe that the moral and ethical standards of business executives are high or very high." Students have a distorted notion of the profits made by a typical large national corporation. The median average of their estimates is 45 percent. The college population has an equally distorted idea of the cost of labor, represented in the purchase price of such products as refrigerators and automobiles. The median average of college responses is 33 percent more than double the actual amount. College education needs to be followed by two or three years of practical experience in the plant manufacturing areas where the work is and where the money has to be generated.

Chapter 18

Trenton Engine was expanded to become one of the largest machining and assembly plants in the Chrysler Corporation. Our break-even point was somewhere between 18 and 20 million dollars per month. When our volume was up during 1968 and 1969 our performance was poor. We worked continuous overtime with new labor, new supervision, inadequate supply of tools and other materials. Lack of running time was a major problem. When the volume was low (1970-71) we laid off the new labor and new supervisors and had fewer tool shortages. We had the same amount of down time but needed less running time, so our performance was better. Getting good performance out of all phases of a machine and assembly plant operation in the production area is no easy task. From the production superintendents down through the production foremen they are all held *accountable* to accomplish results that will pay for the overhead and generate the profit margin that is required. No other element of the plant is held as responsible as a production supervisor.

I am not ignoring the need of good maintenance, which of

course is essential. However, it is the production supervisors who are held *accountable* for productivity, housekeeping, scrap, repair, and quality. Until the recent cutbacks the front office had a large staff just checking to see that production supervisors did their jobs. Personnel, industrial engineering, and some other departments were terrific at finding work for someone else to do—this always reminds me of the corporate staffs. They try to justify their existence by coming up with ways to keep the plant safe, clean, and efficient. They were not capable of executing these ideas, but it always looked easy as long as they were not held *accountable*. They could always be critical. Many foremen, general foremen, and superintendents were demoted for failure to obtain the desired results. We could have saved a great deal of money had the same *accountability* been required from all other departments, including the corporate staffs.

In 1972 our volume started to rise again, and our plant manager was transferred to Air-Temp. Our manufacturing manager became plant manager. A new manufacturing manager was appointed, not a production expert but an excellent engine man—he had worked with the forge and foundry plants. He had a broad variety of experience, including time as resident engineer at the Trenton plant. My opinion was that the new plant manager had selected a well-qualified man. Our volume continued to rise through 1973. Overtime was continuous through the first three quarters of the 1974 model year. The new manfacturing manager was an inspirational-type leader. He was exceptionally helpful in improving the quality of incoming material. The plant manager spent a lot of time out in the plant. I am sure he was well aware of our problems. He never questioned our determination or effort, but he was critical of how we handled our supervisors—he did not think we were rough enough. The job-enrichment technique was for the hourly-rated employee.

In 1969 I moved my family to Trenton. There wasn't any question that this was where I would end my career; regardless of my achievements, I had been passed up for promotion about ten times. Once you have twenty-five years of your life in one corporation, it is difficult to leave; also it was my feeling that I had reached a capacity where I could be extremely competent. My remaining desire was to reach the top of my grade. It was my opinion that men are promoted beyond their capacity and become a burden. Incompetence is created by promoting an individual to a position he or she is incapable of handling. My superiors were aware that I had no desire for promotion but had a strong desire to reach the top of my grade. On the lower executive level from grade nine through eighteen, where most of us had to work our way up, the compensations and promotions were hard to come by. Many of the high-paying positions on the upper staffs were filled off the street; few were ever taken out of the plant. As you can tell by the annual report for 1974, we must have picked up either the inexperienced men or castoffs from other plants. What other conclusion can anyone draw from $11 billion in sales resulting in $52 million in loss?

I was a very loyal employee to the Chrysler Corporation. My purchases of Chrysler-made cars were as follows: 1939, new Dodge; 1940, new DeSoto; 1948, new DeSoto; 1953, new DeSoto; 1956, used DeSoto; 1960, new DeSoto. From that time on I have used Chrysler lease cars. I would not allow my children to purchase any make but Chrysler as long as their bread and butter originated there. Many of my relatives changed from competitors' cars to Chrysler because of my position with Chrysler.

During the years 1972 and 1973 Chrysler appeared to be making a comeback. When Chrysler ended up with a profit, the upper staff levels thought they were doing a tremendous job. Sometimes our profits were one cent on the sales dollar, while our competitors were from five cents to eight cents on the sales dollar. Our officers took the position that these key men, as they refer to themselves, must be paid high salaries and big bonuses, plus stock options, to keep them with the company. It should be clear to us shareholders that most of them should have been released and replaced by men who knew how to make at least five cents on the sales dollar. We have men who are capable of accomplishing this, but unfortunately they won't get the chance until we remove those now in control.

During 1972, 1973, and 1974, Chrysler spent excessive amounts of money on planning for the future. We had a double manufacturing engineering staff. They spent most of their time estimating new projects, most of which were scrapped after excessive costs were incurred. We considered a four-cylinder engine, even sent some of our people to France with the idea of building their four-cylinder engine over here. As usual, we spent a lot of money, then dropped the project. During this period of time, equipment on the floor suffered. The manufacturing engineering help was all tied up on projects. There wasn't anyone available to help on the daily production problems.

I lived close to the plant and made it a point to spend some Saturdays and Sundays in the plant. This habit paid big dividends for the plant many times. I made the decisions to send the departments home because of malfunction that otherwise would have collected premium time costing Trenton Engine thousands of dollars; I also authorized the call in of maintenance to get equipment going for Monday, which saved thousands of dollars. This was expected of me. I was *accountable.*

During high-volume years on three shifts, my production supervisory staff numbered 165 salaried personnel, including 11 executives. The hourly-rated numbered approximately 3,000. At no time did we hold up an assembly plant for lack of engines. When I retired on March 31, 1975, after nine years as manufacturing general superintendent, grade thirteen, my salary was still below midpoint of the grade. A real good example of "job enrichment," wasn't it?

As you have read in the introduction, my duties were no different from any other production executive's—I will qualify that by saying top-level production executives. Several production executives reported to me from all shifts. My day, unlike that of the upper-staff executives, didn't start with a cup of coffee and a *Wall Street Journal* or the daily paper. There was no gathering to discuss the previous day's country club activities, there were no problems such as trying to decide what to do today to attempt to justify my existence. Starting time at Trenton Engine was 7:30 a.m. My routine was quite repetitive. Arriving at my office at 7:20 a.m., I checked the inventories with regards to parts machined at Trenton; if shortages existed, I immediately notified the superintendent of six- and eight-cylinder assembly lines so that he could revise his build schedules; next, reviewed third-shift productivity with the shift superintendent; read the log book covering general information regarding activities of the second shift; checked with the manpower coordinator as to manpower status and advised him of the action he should take in the event he was in trouble due to absenteeism or had excess manpower due to exceptionally good attendance. The assembly lines had top priority; they must run even if it meant shutting down machining departments to man the assembly lines which was the case many times. Since all the departmental managers were fighting for performance, the decision to shut down their departments had to come from me. I would take a walk through the plant, checking the problem areas; superintendents, general foremen, foremen, and hourly-rated employees greeted me with problems that would adversely affect the performance for the day. Many were repetitive: machines down, fixtures inoperative, tool shortages, lack of maintenance coverage, and vendor stock problems. It was enough to make a grown man cry. Returning to my office, I evaluated the problems, usually making calls to the tool stores, cutter grind, production control, quality control, and tool research. Most of these departments had already been contacted by my production staff. My calls added emphasis to the seriousness of the problems.

A maintenance meeting was held in my office each morning

at 8:30 a.m. All service departments were represented. Production superintendents reported on items that had to be taken care of immediately. Plans of action and specific assignments were made; by this time it was 9:10 a.m. The daily plant manager's executive staff meeting was held in the executive conference room. The previous day's performance was reviewed. Other information or communications of importance were generally discussed at this meeting. The length of the meeting ran from fifteen minutes to an hour and a half. Some specific assignments were made. I was often reminded that direct labor was holding back the progress of the plant. Since it was the only department that was measured, it was the only department held *accountable.* No one really had any way of knowing how inefficient or overmanned the other departments were. How simple it was to say *get direct labor* on schedule, but how difficult it was to come up with anything constructive to assist me in the task of accomplishing the desired results!

I would return to my office, check the production counts, have my clerk check previous day variance hours by department, and then call in my production superintendents for a staff meeting. In the production staff meeting, any communication or information that I received in the plant manager's meeting was conveyed. We would review the daily forecast and make the necessary moves to get the best performance. I want to emphasize at this point that during the time I was manufacturing general superintendent, no plant in the auto industry could have had a more conscientious staff of production clerks, although their work load was tremendous. Effort and attendance were excellent; my clerk was like my right arm.

After the production staff meeting I would make another tour of the plan, after which I went home to lunch. A quality audit meeting immediately followed lunch. Variance, tool usage, scrap and miscellaneous meetings, plus housekeeping tours mixed in with serious breakdowns and shortages, left no time for coffee breaks for the rest of the first shift. At the end of the shift, departments that missed their targets would hold a meeting, each supervisor being held *accountable* for his area. Explanations for variance were submitted to my office before the supervisors went home—this would be approximately 4:00 p.m.

In the meantime, second-shift superintendents were being lined up—their last stop would be my office. I would brief them personally on anything of extreme importance. I would make my final summary to the manufacturing manager's office, usually between 5:00 and 6:00 p.m. I gathered up the papers I hadn't had time to read during the day—they would be read sometime before morning. Time flew—where did the day go? There was never a dull day, never a day with enough time in it to get done all of the work that had to be done. Unlike a staff position where time drags because of no activity, the Trenton plant production executives were blessed with enough work to keep them from becoming bored. Time never drags for any one who is in charge of a production division.

Other activities where my production staff performed the lion's share of the work were soliciting for donors in the blood bank drives, buyers for U. S. savings bond drives, and contributors in the United Fund drives. The upper echelon set all the targets; all my staff had to do was pressure the supervisory and hourly employees into participation. There wasn't any question about my own contribution as far as the United Fund or political contribution was concerned: the upper echelon established the formula on how much I was to contribute to the foundation and how much I was to contribute to a political party of my choice.

The plant manager insisted on getting the amount as set forth in the formula; while I deeply resented this, I always gave the amount requested. In 1974 Ford Motor Company and General Motors discontinued the practice of requiring the executives to make political contributions. Chrysler had to be different—they insisted on collecting the political contributions for 1974. Of course, when they lost money on sales of $11 billion, it was plain they were not very *accountable* for other people's money, either.

———————Chapter 19———————

Many shareholders will question how the plants were able to run with so much mismanagement at the upper level. We had our problems at the plants—it was a never-ending battle to try to meet all the targets set forth by the budget department. We had considerable trouble with loss of running time due to machine malfunction. We had trouble controlling scrap and repair costs and many other miscellaneous problems. In this chapter some of the communications and action taken to meet our targets are on record. They were routine procedure fully understood by people who spend their lives in manufacturing plants. Remember when you read the communications that they covered a period of time during which we built and sold 12,033,267 engines.

Shareholders invest in a company with the full knowledge that there is a possibility of losing. Most shareholders don't care too much about the operations of a company as long as it makes money and pays a dividend, but when you lose money because of poor management it's like giving your money away. Many shareholders, when they read this book, will recognize that one can invest in a good company and still lose money if the company is mismanaged. For those of you who are interested in the inner operations of a corporation you have an investment in, I will outline what happened at Trenton Engine Plant.

Trenton Engine Plant was divided into eighteen production departments. These were divided to form five divisions. The assembly division was the largest division with regards to manpower. Each division was managed by a production executive. The executive was a superintendent, grade ten. Each superintendent had a supervisory staff of general foremen, who were referred to as departmental managers. Depending on the size of the area, each departmental manager had from two to four or more foremen reporting to him. We tried to hold our foremen to a ratio of one in twenty; in other words, each supervisor in the machine shop had approximately twenty employees, while on the assembly lines there was one foreman to every thirty-five employees. The capacity of the eight-cylinder machining departments was quoted at 3,000 engines per day on a straight time basis. The capacity of the six-cylinder machining departments was quoted as 1,800 engines per day on a straight time basis. To get the capacity, the machine shop had to run three shifts in most departments. The assembly lines could produce this capacity on two shifts. Every time we had a change in schedule, we would have a manpower shuffle throughout the plant. During the time when I was general superintendent of manufacturing, the schedule varied from 1,800 six-cylinder engines per day to a low of 500 engines per day, and the eight-cylinder engines from a high of 3,000 to a low of 800 engines per day. When I left in March 1975 we were producing 1,250 six-cylinder engines and 900 eight-cylinder engines per day. Because of the variation of requirements, which resulted in many manpower changes, we incurred three major problems: production loss during training periods, excessive scrap, and repairs, which also had a serious effect with regard to quality. I am fully aware that all automobile plants have requirement variations. Good planning management reduces these changes to a minimum. We at Trenton Engine had seven line-speed changes in three months. No one with any experience in building automobiles could give our corporate planning department any credit for *accountability*. The engine plants were kept in a constant turmoil, not knowing from one day to the next what the schedule was going to be. Every line-speed change cost a great deal of money. The corporate officers recognized the cost and allowed the plant launching money for each line-speed change. Now, since the corporate financial condition is so critical, the launching money has been discontinued, and the cost is just another item the plant performance has to absorb.

Each department has a scrap target. When I discussed this item, no one would believe what it cost Chrysler shareholders. We have two passenger car engine plants in the United States, Mound Road and Trenton. At Trenton our scrap cost during low volume ran about $35,000 per week, at high volume about $65,000 per week. My supervisory staff and I tried every method we knew to control this waste. We made some progress, but I am convinced no company can control scrap costs unless incoming rough stock from the various vendors categorically honors the material specifications. Our own forge and foundries were the worst offenders.

The second major problem was the condition of equipment. Much of the equipment was in need of replacement and another large percentage of it in need of repair. Buying new equipment or making costly repairs was the responsibility of the powers above me. I could only make recommendations. When top management is squeezing the plant for all they can get out of it, recommendations that cost money fall on deaf ears most of the time. It was a constant battle to try to stop the scrap. Our degree of success depended upon recognizing the real problems and being willing to spend the money to replace or repair the equipment. Failure to keep equipment in good operating condition also caused another big expensive waste of manpower and performance—repairs were excessive.

When the repair bank is high, the scrap rate is high. We worked night and day to get defective material repaired. We were well aware that to stop defective material at the source was the real solution to reduce the repair bank. It was very serious in many ways: one, it created excessive inventory that ran into millions of dollars; two, extra manpower required to repair the defective material cost millions of dollars. The equipment didn't get bad overnight; we had built 12 million engines on this equipment. We had no preventive main-tenance program. Remember that the upper echelon con-trolled the money to replace or rebuild equipment. It would be poor management to blame the failure of the scrap and repair programs on production supervisors and their employees. Our inability to control these two items seriously affected quality and plant performance. My production team was a proud one—they worked with me many extra hours and went home at night deeply depressed. It was a never-ending battle still going on when I retired; however, much of the six-cylinder equipment is being replaced at this time. My point is we would have saved millions of dollars if the top officers had acted five years sooner. Supervisory production out on the floor and the front office were like two different worlds. In the production area each supervisor was held *accountable*. They all knew someone would be on their backs all the time unless they kept the departments clean and made an honest effort to meet the work standards and above all to meet the planned performance target for the day. In the front office no such targets were set. It always seemed to me that the attitude was:"What's the rush? What we don't do today we'll do tomorrow."

Tool cribs were located in the plant. The supervisors and follow-up men were located in the front office. When there were no tools available, production supervisors were in se-rious trouble. Calls to the tool supervisor for information as to when tools would be available always received the answer, "Let me check and I will call you back." Often the return call, usually from one to two hours later, would report no tools available until next week or next month. Orders had been placed but not received; there were also other reasons, but the fact remained we were still out of tools. Tool research got into the act and tried to come with a substitution. Our tool supply system just did not work the way it was supposed to work: most of our tool boards were empty, and our tool floats were never balanced. We were short of something at all times. In spite of this, tool stores were over their budget and the inventory dollar value was too high; they had to reduce the dollar value. This was done by scrapping new tools where the usage was low and the inventory high. The loss of productivity caused by our inability to control usage and availability cost shareholders millions of dollars. *Accountability* is still lacking in this area.

I will outline what happened at Trenton Engine Plant with regard to the number of engines built there from 1957, when I first started there, up to 1974, and the major changes made to the engines. Following are eight-cylinder and six-cylinder engines built from 1957 to 1974:

Model Year	8-Cylinder	6-Cylinder	Total
1957 "K" Series	9,858	0	9,858
1958 "L" Series	99,202	0	99,202
1959 "M" Series	198,657	0	198,657
1960 "P" Series	179,142	411,680	590,822
1961 "R" Series	134,051	388,130	522,231
1962 "S" Series	184,377	372,582	556,960
1963 "T" Series	212,617	526,993	739,610
1964 "V" Series	277,164	546,788	823,952
1965 "A" Series	471,132	421,437	892,619
1966 "B" Series	541,184	362,637	903,811
1967 "C" Series	517,220	280,000	797,220
1968 "D" Series	708,710	299,868	1,008,578
1969 "E" Series	750,984	253,316	1,004,300
1970 "F" Series	577,496	279,223	856,719
1971 "G" Series	369,687	291,165	660,852
1972 "H" Series	409,148	336,813	745,991
1973 "J" Series	552,836	357,744	910,620
1974 Model	311,540	399,725	711,265
Total	6,505,005	5,528,262	12,033,267

June 1957—Build out power steering
June 1957—Launched "B" engine
February 1958—Launched 6-cylinder, 230-cubic-inch engine
June 1958—Launched "RB" engine
November 1958—M & I moved to Jefferson
July 1959—Launched V/8 truck engine
August 1964—"A" Series 170 cubic-inch engine to Canada
July 1965—Build out 413 passenger car engine
July 1965—Launched 440 passenger car engine
July 1966—Build out 361 passenger car engine
July 1967—"D" Series—new pistons and cylinder heads all V/8 passenger car-type engines, new 6-cylinder crank
July 1968—"E" Series—new intake manifold V/8 truck 6-cylinder stamped impeller, water pump, new exhaust 440-cubic-inch, 3-2 barrel carburetor introduced late "E" series
July 1969—"F" Series—new intake and exhaust manifolds all passenger cars—6-cylinder exhaust—new V/8 piston
July 1970—"G" Series new parts—8-cylinder, cylinder head RB intake manifold—piston—camshaft—6-cylinder camshaft
July 1971—"H" Series new parts—8-cylinder 400-cubic-inch engine B and RB pistons—vibration dampers—intake and exhaust manifolds—California roller chain camshaft drive all trucks, all distributors—6-cylinder intake manifolds—cylinder heads—California all distributors—exhaust valve seat—induction harden
July 1972-1973 model new parts—6-cylinder intake and exhaust manifold—distributors and wiring—cylinder head cover—oil pan—8-cylinder intake and exhaust manifold—distributors and wiring—water pump housing—fuel pump—400- and 440-cubic-inch blocks running change late 1972 model—oil pan, cylinder head cover—PEGR valves
August 1973-1974 model new parts—6-cylinder intake mani-shafts—cylinder head covers 6-cylinder—crankshafts and

intake manifolds—water pump body—PEGR valves—crank-shafts—cylinder head covers 6-cylinder—crankshafts and "C" body oil pan

August 1974-1975 model new parts—6-cylinder distributor-cylinder head—clutch housing—spark plugs and cables—exhaust valves—8-cylinder B and RB intake and exhaust manifolds—passenger car engines—PEGR valves—distribu-tors—cylinder heads—exhaust valves—B and RB blocks—RB 50,000-mile spark plug

Chapter 20

We at plant level, while controlled to a great extent by corporate direction, could have improved our performance by doing a better job in a number of areas, but like the higher echelon we didn't take drastic action until the world came tumbling down around us. When you get desperate you find out you can do a lot of things that otherwise seem impractical. I don't mean to imply that we were not always trying to meet or beat our profit plans. We knew improvement in tools and equipment was necessary to have an efficient plant. My production executives also knew that we must get the best out of what we had. Our attitude had to be that there wasn't anything we couldn't do. I couldn't let them believe the job couldn't be done, regardless of the problems. I wrote the following communications to try to eliminate negative thinking and motivate aggressive action to get the best out of what we had to work with. One of our methods of being sure our employees were fully aware of their responsibilities was to issue memos that each employee either read or had read to him or her. Most employees signed; some refused to sign, and it was so marked on the communication.

Communication #1 was as follows:

Date _____

Dept._____ Badge _____ Employee _____

The above employee has been instructed by his supervisor with regard to the following items:

1. WORK STANDARDS (attainable and net)   _____
2. TOOL CHANGE AND GAGING
   FREQUENCIES   _____
3. WEARING SAFETY GLASSES   _____
4. DEVELOPING SAFE WORK HABITS   _____
5. HOUSEKEEPING (keeping stock and
   garbage off floor and in proper containers) _____
6. ATTENDANCE (absenteeism and
   tardiness)   _____
7. STARTING, QUITTING, AND
   RELIEF TIME   _____
8. DEFECTIVE WORKMANSHIP (generat-
   ing scrap and repairs)   _____

The above employee has been informed that failure to make a sincere effort to comply with these instructions could result in disciplinary action.

Manufacturing General Superintendent

We were having a considerable amount of trouble controlling scrap. Communication #2 was written to all production supervisors:

Subject: SCRAP REDUCTION

Our efforts to date have failed to accomplish the desired results. An analysis of our problems reveals the following facts and necessary corrective action to be taken:

A. Most departments could have an acceptable scrap

71

level by controlling three or four operations which consistently generate scrap.

B. An operator who makes a lot of scrap in one day is generally identified, and where negligence is established, corrective action is taken.

C. An operator who makes a little bit of scrap every day through carelessness is not identified and there is no corrective action taken.

D. The daily small scrap makers are generating the largest portion of the total scrap.

E. It becomes obvious that to reduce scrap we must immediately develop methods to identify parts by stamping or color coding, which will reveal the operation, operator, and shift generating the scrap.

F. When color coding or stamping methods of identification have been established, it must be broadcast to the inspection department so that when writing up scrap they can transfer this information to the scrap ticket.

G. When the production supervisor reviews and signs the scrap ticket, he will record the scrap along with the identity of the operator.

H. Reviewing weekly totals will highlight the seriousness of the operator who makes a little scrap every day. We will be able to take and support whatever corrective action is necessary. This should help enforce proper tool change and gaging frequencies.

Production machining superintendents must have scrap identification and recording program in effect by 10-66.

A copy of the previous day's itemized scrap recording must be submitted to my office each morning at the 8:30 meetings.

An itemized repair report must also be submitted at the 8:30 meetings.

All production supervision must extend the necessary

efforts and determination to reduce scrap and repairs 100%. *PARTICIPATION IS MANDATORY.*

Six months later, after many meetings and different approaches, we were still in trouble. Communication #3 was issued, which covered four major subjects and was issued to all production supervision.

Communication #3:
ALL PRODUCTION SUPERVISORS

A review of the last six (6) months' activity indicates:
(A) That our direct labor performance has not met plan.
(B) Our safety record is much worse than previous year.
(C) Housekeeping, while improving, leaves much to be desired.
(D) Scrap reduction program has made very little progress.
We cannot meet our targets when supervisors ignore the very basic fundamentals of good supervision. To be appraised and meet job requirement, a supervisor must be sure that his work force:
   (1) (a) Starts on time and does not quit early;
      (b) does not overstay relief periods;
      (c) keeps work area clean;
      (d) works safely and observes all safety rules;
      (e) meets work standards;
      (f) changes tools and gage parts on proper established frequency;
      (g) comes to work when scheduled on time.
   (2) Observation reveals that many supervisors are not making the necessary effort with regard to the subjects listed.
   (3) Controlling these items is the direct responsibility of the supervisor.
   (4) We cannot tolerate any supervisor who does not put forth a determined effort to fulfill his responsibilities.

(5) Our targets can be met. The desired results will be accomplished by aggressive action and determination.

(6) Immediate response to enforce good operating procedure is mandatory.

Manufacturing General Superintendent

In 1968 our volume had increased drastically, but it was difficult to hire and hold good labor. We continued to pound away at the everyday problems. I wrote a memo called "Cost Reduction," which covered a very broad area of the production operation. I wrote many communications but am highlighting only a few in this book.

Communication # 4—To all supervision
Subject: *COST REDUCTION PROGRAM*

Cost reduction is accomplished by action, determination, and a sincere and honest effort by all concerned. In order to obtain the desired results it is mandatory for supervision to participate to the fullest extent and to encourage your hourly-rated employees' participation as much as possible.

Listed below are a few items which must be worked on to reduce cost:

1. Reduce scrap and repairs.
2. Enforce work standards.
3. Tool change frequency and gaging frequencies should be strictly adhered to.
4. Instruct and enforce all good housekeeping and safety rules.
5. Properly instruct new operators on all phases of their jobs.
6. New methods and ideas.
7. Combining of operations or possible change of sequence.

8. New tools.
9. All machines should be brought up to proper cycle time.
10. Reduce tool and fixture breakage.
11. Reduce oil usage.
12. Utilization of manpower, absentees, late starts, early quits, overstaying of relief, etc.

Most of the above-listed items are not new, but our progress has not been satisfactory. *We must search for new ideas to solve these old problems!*

We must make good use of data issued by budget, quality control, and industrial engineering as:
1. Cycle counts and adjustments.
2. High tool cost items.
3. High tool breakage items.
4. Hydraulic oil usage.
5. Machine cycle checks and work samples.
6. Safety reports.
7. Non-standard manpower status.
8. Inspection, final teardown report (listing major defects)
9. Scrap and performance charts.

Each supervisor must have a specific task to reduce the cost permanently on some item in his area each week. Planning and organizing this task force, *holding each supervisor responsible for action and progress, should get the best results.* Other types of approaches usually get much conversation but little action.

TO BE RATED AS A GOOD PRODUCTION TEAM WE MUST GET ON PLAN, REDUCE OUR SCRAP AND REPAIRS, SO LET'S GET STARTED AND GET THE RESULTS ALL OF US ARE CAPABLE OF.

Each area superintendent will hold weekly meetings. *The minutes must be recorded and all progress on cost reduction in your area must be included in your weekly progress report to me. This report is to be in my office by 2:00 p.m. every Tuesday.*

Manufacturing General Superintendent

Communication #5

PLANS TO IMPROVE DIRECT LABOR PERFORMANCE

1. Train general foremen and foremen to do a better job of planning and using methods which will develop the proper attitude and obtain a fair day's work out of each employee.
2. Program equipment to maintenance for correction of defective fixtures and quality problems.
3. Have general foreman of each area outline program for progress and forecast improvement trend.
4. Hold weekly scrap and repair meetings and follow up action to reduce same.
5. Enforce tool change and gaging frequencies.
6. Set up action program to correct slow cycle times.
7. Have supervisors report on pieces produced during available running time rather than how much they lost due to down time.
8. Each superintendent will review hourly counts as often as time permits and move fast to correct bad counts.

Manufacturing General Superintendent

Quality, scrap, and repairs always run hand in hand—to control one you have to control them all. On December 12, 1970, a communication was written to the quality control manager regarding scrap identification. There were five pages showing how scrap would be identified by shift, operation, and operator. The letter covering the identification package reads as follows:

76

Communication #6
Subject: Scrap Identification

Our scrap reduction program requires positive identification of parts as to shift, operation, and operator. This information must be transferred to scrap tickets. Scrap writer should also separate scrap by shift for supervisors' and operators' review. This must be done on a daily basis.

Production identification of machined parts outlining color codes used and area painted, stamps used and area stamped, is attached.

Every effort must be made to place scrap in proper class:

(A) Operator's negligence.

(B) Machine malfunction.

(C) Vendor.

Production and maintenance will both sign scrap tickets classed as (B) scrap.

Production and inspection will both sign scrap tickets classed as (C) scrap.

No department shall charge scrap to another department without the scrap ticket being signed by the superintendent of the department being charged.

Scrap tickets must be reviewed, signed, and expedited on a daily basis.

Manufacturing General Superintendent

Whenever we would change an identification, we would issue a supplement as follows.

Communication #7
Subject: Scrap Identification
Supplement to letter dated 2-12-70.
Department 0860—Color Identification

1ST SHIFT - YELLOW
2ND SHIFT - GREEN
3RD SHIFT - BLUE

The shafts will be marked in the skid after the assembly of the plug.

Department 5860—Color Identification

Same as department 0860.

Departments 0800 & 5250—Color Identification

1ST SHIFT - RED
2ND SHIFT - BLUE
3RD SHIFT - BLACK

The scrap will be accumulated by shift by the inspector.

All shifts will check one part of each machine, over and above their regular gaging frequency, and place their part next to the machine, with the hour marked on the dome of the piston. The inspector will periodically check these pistons and if satisfied with the quality will place them on the conveyor.

Further, the last piece checked at the end of the shift will be left at the machine and the incoming shift will check this piece and the first piece machined to see if they correspond by size.

Department 5300—Color Identification

1ST SHIFT - BLUE
2ND SHIFT - ORANGE
3RD SHIFT - GREEN

(A) *6-Cylinder Oil Pumps*
    1. The Heald operator will paint on the back of the filter base bowl.
    2. After inspection and OK after the Beach tester the operator will paint the pump on the side of the base.

(B) *6-Cylinder Water Pump*
    1. After inspection and OK the pump will be

painted in back of the goose neck.
Manufacturing General Superintendent

As you can see as you read the communications, many problems were repetitive and much more difficult to solve than it appeared on the surface. In 1969, because we were having considerable trouble machining connecting rods, the superintendent of maintenance and I made a trip to the Ford plant in Lima, Ohio, to review their method of machining some operations in the V/8 connecting rod department. I wrote a letter to the manufacturing manager of our plant regarding our trip and observations. My letter was as follows:

Subject: Trip to Ford Plant, Lima, Ohio, on 4-3-69 to Review Their Methods of Machining Some Operations in the V/8 Connecting Rod departments.

Mr. Cam Roy and I arrived at the plant at 1:00 p.m. Mr. E. Bond, manager of manufacturing engineering, met us in the lobby and escorted us to the chief tool engineer's office. After a brief discussion we toured part of the rod line with Don Shade, their tool process engineer for the rod departments.

In final summary, much of their processing is very good. However, they have a very serious problem with bore size control and bend and twist. We cannot afford to create these same problems.

Our present method of machining V/8 connecting rods leaves much to be desired. It is impossible to machine rods to print specification.

Anyone who would be willing to believe our problems in the rod lines will be over once we get the hones and rebuild the Excellos so that they will rough and finish bore on the same spindles, in my opinion, is very much under the wrong impression.

All the money we spend in the rod line must be to im-

79

prove our methods, to improve our quality and reduce scrap and repairs, thereby increasing our productivity. My recommendations are as follows:

(1) Bolt hole machine on rod should locate from pin hole and be pushed to one side of nest.
(2) Bolt holes on cap must be located by pushing to one side of cap.
(3) Dispose of Footeburt & K. Barnes chamfering machines.
(4) Make rough boring machine out of present Excellos and incorporate chamfering device. Rough bore crank end only.
(5) Finish weight mills should follow this because of our method of handling.
(6) Finish grind thrust face after weight mills.
(7) Finish bore crank and pin end using Cam Roy's concept of holding pin end to eliminate bend and twist problems. Unload by hand and hang on conveyor to hones.
(8) While waiting for delivery of new finish boring machines, fix up Healds and Bryant grinders to act as finish bores. Leave .002 for honing stock.

This method of processing would eliminate much of the repair work and scrap. Quality of rods presented to motor line would be much improved.

Manufacturing General Superintendent

Chapter 21

A group of friends and I attended the stockholders' meeting held in Centerline on April 15, 1975. I taped the entire meeting on my recorder. Chrysler provides a very small facility for such an important meeting. Except for some of the board of directors and officers, the rest of those attending were angry and disgusted shareholders. Regardless of how they felt, there was nothing they could do that would change anything. One could accuse the officers and board of directors of gross mismanagement and with $11 billion in sales, resulting in $52 million in loss, there was no question that mismanagement was the real problem.

The chairman's comments confirmed the fact that he was head of an incompetent organization that really did not discover that they were in trouble until October 1974. It's a pretty sad situation when a company the size of Chrysler has to get desperate before any action is taken. The chairman didn't acknowledge that our competitors had the same difficult times and expenses to deal with; he didn't say because they were *accountable* to their shareholders they managed to make a profit and pay a dividend. He commented that the board of directors did not have to own much Chrysler stock to be competent directors. After reading the proxy statement, which reveals all are successful individuals, one comes to the conclusion that most of them aren't interested in buying stock in a company that pays no dividends or invest in a stock that drops 75 percent in two years. So while they are competent in some fields, they certainly couldn't be considered competent in directing an automobile company to $11 billion in sales which ended up with $52 million in loss. The chairman told the shareholders that their officers had now taken the necessary action to bring the company back into a profitable status.

My executive status with Chrysler terminated March 31, 1975—thirty-eight and a half years, of which twelve years were spent in an executive capacity. My position is that Chrysler made most of its own problems. In my opinion, nothing was done in October that couldn't have been done five years sooner, when we were making one cent on the sales dollar and should have been making five cents on the sales dollar. Fellow shareholders, with good management we could possibly receive dividends of from two dollars to four dollars per year. To my knowledge, Chrysler was never competitive with Ford or General Motors, as far as profit on the sales dollar is concerned, as long as I was with Chrysler. As soon as we started making money, top officers and key men would start adding to their staff—all had big ideas that cost nothing but money.

Seventeen percent of the market, *properly managed,* would make plenty of profit for Chrysler, raise the share value, and start paying dividends again. We must change our top management to one more knowledgeable about running an automobile industry. If we don't move fast, I predict no profits this year and most likely no dividends for at least two years.

The chairman stated that in excess of 40 million shares were represented at this meeting. After collection of the few votes that were cast by the angry and dissatisfied shareholders who were present, the results were read off: in excess of 38 million were in favor of retaining the present board and officers, about 5 percent were opposed. I am sure the proxy votes had established the outcome long before the meeting started. The chairman reported, "You have just elected your board of directors and officers for the coming year."

After about two hours of question-and-answer session, the meeting was adjourned. I am sure that many of those 38 million shareholders were very disappointed in the management of Chrysler performances for 1974, but the corporation method of soliciting votes by proxy, encouraging the shareholders to vote for them and anything they recommend, gives them an advantage which is almost unbeatable— the majority votes as the proxy recommends. But don't forget, fellow shareholders, we own Chrysler, and this company has been in and out of trouble for the last fifteen years. It's time we joined together to select a management group that will work for the people who own the company, a management team that will recognize the contributions of the individuals who make the company successful and compensate them properly, be they hourly or on salary. This management team must not be indecisive, it must be *accountable* and move rapidly to separate the men from the boys. This can be done with enough shareholders' determination and effort. Start the snowball rolling, watch the momentum.

When I left the corporation on March 31 we had millions of dollars worth of six-cylinder equipment in the plant but weren't allowed any money to install it. We had spent a lot of money planning on a four-cylinder motor and then dropped the project—now, with the public and shareholders yelling for action, they will be going all out to put a sub-compact on the market. The choice machine builders are already working or our competitors' new equipment, so as usual Chrysler will end up paying second-choice vendors premium time to build equipment which at its best will be a rush order of equipment of questionable quality.

------------*Chapter 22*------------

No matter how we criticize the officers and board of directors, we know none will resign, so we are stuck for at least another year.

So what can be done while we work out a way to replace them next year? I suggest the following:

1. Reduce the burden to a minimum. I don't mean just clerks, typists and telephone operators. I mean about sixty percent of the upper staffs, including about fifty percent of the vice presidents.

2. Stop the giveaway programs that go on in our plants. Our competitors have less union representation and get more work out of employees. The loopholes in our contract prevent this. To work five men on Saturday, for instance, we must bring in

four or five union stewards and committeemen to stand around and watch them.

3. Stop the loose expense accounts and country club memberships, at least until we are competitive with Ford and General Motors.

4. Stop recruiting college grads.

5. Start being fair with the plant production personnel, where the money has to be made. Compensate them in line with our competitors—they are the key men we should be trying to hold. Statements such as "all cost-of-living allowances to be discontinued for non-union employees and stock-thrift plan discontinued" are very detrimental to supervisory morale. This kind of treatment will never create the aggressiveness required to turn this company around. We can't pay our hourly employees more than we pay our supervisors.

6. Change the vacations method by following the example of other successful companies, by shutting down from two to four weeks and letting the employees and supervisors get their vacations out of the way. We all know the expense of new hires for the summer.

7. Lease cars to all supervisors who desire them—this would be a profitable venture.

8. Encourage the news media to stop highlighting the percentage of unemployed and report the high percentage that is employed and urge the employed to do their part by spending to get the unemployed back to work.

10. In January we shut the plant down and sent the employees home for a week. Today (May 1975) we are running departments overtime and paying premium time—also the cost-of-living increase makes labor higher now than in January. Planning *accountability*? There isn't any.

11. We get more bad publicity than any of our competitors, so why not hire someone who can improve our image? Articles such as the following only open up criticism for our management:

1. *Detroit News* article March 28, 1975, in large print:

"Chrysler Sees Brighter Future." The chairman of the board made the following points:

Layoffs of 15,000 more white-collar workers since last October are now considered permanent and have permitted the company to strengthen its financial position.

Question: Why were they on the payroll in the first place?

The Jefferson Avenue assembly plant probably will keep going at least through next year.

Question: If it is not making the required profit margin, why is it operating at all?

The financial outlook is that the company will make money this year.

Question: When will the favorability start? ($116 million loss in the first quarter narrowed to $94 million after adjustments.)

The industry should have a very good year in 1976.

I noticed you didn't name Chrysler, and you must be including foreign-made cars, which are having a very good year this year.

The number-three auto maker will remain in competition with Ford Motor Company and General Motors Corporation.

Question: When do you think we can get into their league?

The chairman said Chrysler has now completed its major program to cut overhead and operating costs.

It took us five months to do what we could have done five years ago, and you're still carrying a lot of deadwood.

Other news reports that are detrimental and damage our public relations are as follows:

"Cars still in post-rebate slide, imports up 13 percent from last year." Article in *Detroit Free Press,* April 4, 1975.

Chrysler is the only company to continue the rebate. "Chrysler sales off 32 percent." *Detroit Free Press*, April 4, 1975.

I have twenty articles from either the *Free Press* or the *Detroit News* that I feel cause a negative reaction from the buying public.

"Chrysler loss worst ever" in large print, front page of the *Detroit Free Press.* Same paper, page five, in large print: "Chrysler loss worst of Chrysler's fifty-year history."

"Auto firms blamed for sales slump," *Detroit News,* May 7, 1975.

"British Chrysler Corp. warns of total shutdown." *Detroit Free Press*, June 23, 1975.

"California Air Board orders Chrysler to begin recall." *Detroit Free Press,* May 21, 1975.

"U. S.-made cars fell 26 percent in April, while import sales rose the same amount." (*I wonder what our management is doing to curb this problem!*)

"Final Forecast," *Detroit News* article, May 2, 1975. "Chrysler will lose 60 million in second quarter while Ford earns 75 million and General Motors earns 300 million."

"Chrysler talks hopefully as analysts forecast trouble!" *Detroit Free Press*, May 22, 1975.

May 24, *Detroit News,* large-print, front-page article: "Better days ahead, G. M. stockholders told." (*It was an interesting stockholders' meeting. The stockholders of General Motors and Ford haven't had to tolerate bad management—if they weren't receiving a good dividend each quarter, the top officers wouldn't be in office long.*

"U.S. buys Soviet tractors, 3,000 ordered at $8,000 each." *Detroit Free Press*, April 22, 1975. (*My comment: Maybe we should build tractors!*)

Fellow shareholders, this only proves that our present management can't cope with today's problems. We have already dropped from fifth largest corporation to eleventh. In this book I haven't discussed problems caused by government regulations and high cost of labor and materials because it has been my opinion that our competitors face the same conditions. As each day goes by and new articles come to my attention, the loss of public confidence and acceptability looms greater and greater. It makes me fearful that we shareholders may not be able to change management fast enough to regain a favorable image.

The article in *Fortune* magazine, May 1975, regarding Chrysler should be of special interest to Chrysler shareholders: "Many of our top officers have held their positions a long time. Well, it's time to stop playing musical chairs and put some fresh blood in those chairs." A *Detroit News* article on May 25: "Ford to produce own mini-cars, challenge to imports promised." The president of Ford Motor Company knows how to manage an automobile company. The public has confidence in the top management of our main competitors. *Nothing* could change the future of Chrysler faster than to be able to read in large print: *"CHRYSLER CHANGES TOP MANAGEMENT. New Group of Manufacturing Management Appointed. Accountability and Public Confidence Will Be Restored."* This would be the best headline possible to answer the question millions of people ask, "What's wrong with Chrysler?" But it will not happen unless we shareholders force the action.

The 25 percent pay cut the top officers took for the

months of December 1974 through March 1975 didn't cause any hardship on the upper echelon. In order to understand this, you have to be familiar with the executive bonus program. When a bonus is paid, as it was in 1972 and 1973, the executives get their award as follows: In 1972, for example, the top offices received bonuses from $50,000 up to and in excess of $200,000. In the event they stayed on the payroll through December 31, 1972, they received 40 percent of their award in March 1973. They received the balance in three equal installments in January of the following years: 1974, 1975, and 1976. So the 1972 award of $200,000 would equal $80,000 to be paid in March 1973 and $40,000 in January 1974, 1975, and 1976. Now let us take the same executive and assume his bonus of $200,000 in 1972 is the same in 1973—he would receive $40,000 in January 1974 and $80,000 in March 1974. No bonus award was granted for 1974, but he still receives a carry-over from 1972 and 1973 of $40,000 for each year, payable in January 1975. He will still get the carry-over of $40,000 for 1972 and 1973 in January 1976. Carry-over from 1973 of $40,000 would be paid in January 1977. Of course, he has to qualify by being on the payroll through those years.

Not so with the executives of the plants, where the money has to be generated. Trenton plant executives were in the range of $4,000 to $10,000 and there wasn't much of a carry-over to offset their cut in pay. Prudent management cut out the dividends, but as you can see they didn't cut out their carry-over bonuses or stock options. It proves that the one area where management is very *accountable* is in taking care of itself.

When the chairman made the statement to the shareholders at the stockholders' meeting about the top officers taking a 25 percent pay cut for four months, he didn't mention the carry-over bonuses they will be collecting each January through 1977. They also commented on one member of the board of directors who is president of the University of Michigan. The university purchased some vehicles from Chrysler, and to eliminate any conflict of interest he donated his board salary of $7,500 to the university. He didn't mention that four of the biggest vendors servicing Chrysler have a man on the board of directors, and they are also on the incentive compensation committee.

Why don't we have a sub-compact car on the market now? No reason but the lack of *accountability* on the part of the top officers. They wasted enough money at Trenton to pay a large part of the expense. They installed a new crankshaft line and then decided we didn't need it, so the equipment was moved out. I don't know how much money was lost on that venture. They did the excavating to install a new assembly line, which was another total loss. We had to refill the area and pour new cement. I understand the loss was $300,000.

Every company makes mistakes, but when you make so many that $11 billion in sales results in $52 million in loss, we have to face up to the facts. All indications point to a company going nowhere because of mismanagement.

Appointments to a high position because of whom you know rather than what you know puts square pegs in round holes. In my opinion, this great corporation will never be really successful until the square pegs are removed and replaced with management that knows how to run an automobile manufacturing company.

I repeat that stockholders own this company. Through our organized and aggressive action, we can gather enough support to turn this company into one that will regain its rightful position in the automobile world. We must be held *accountable* to make the next stockholders' meeting more than a formality.

The stockholders' meeting ended with a question-and-answer session, so I feel it appropriate to finish my book in that manner.

Chapter 23

Questions and Answers

Questions were submitted to me by various groups of people. The answers are the author's personal opinions based on knowledge acquired during thirty-eight and one-half years with the corporation, the last nine years as general superintendent of manufacturing in a multi-million-dollar operation.

Q. What's wrong with Chrysler?

A. When a company has over $11 billion in sales and loses $52 million while its competitors face the same difficult times, higher costs, and government regulations, General Motors and Ford still made a profit and paid dividends. Chrysler lost money and cut off quarterly dividends. We must remember 1974 was the second-highest sales year in Chrysler history. Mismanagement is the only way this could happen.

Q. How can the top officers be removed?

A. By putting enough unhappy shareholders' shares together, say about 30 million shares. We would be able to make some moves. We can vote them out at the next shareholders' meeting. Just return your proxy instruction card properly marked, dated, and signed, making sure it is returned in time.

Q. How are appointments to high positions made?

A. Sometimes on the basis of ability and knowledge. Many, many times because of knowing the right people. That's how we get the square pegs for the round holes. From personnel manager to board chairman, unqualified selections cost Chrysler millions of dollars.

Q. Why don't we have a sub-compact built in the United States ready to market now?

A. Really, there is no good reason except for bad judgment on the part of the top officers. This is about a minimum two-year project. We should catch up with Ford and General Motors in a couple of years.

Q. What do you think of Chrysler's financial condition?

A. Their latest report to shareholders indicates they have worked up a large source of credit. They cannot borrow money without paying interest.

Q. When do you think Chrysler will pay dividends again?

A. It will not be in 1975. It could be in the last half of 1976; however, I wouldn't count on it.

Q. What has Chrysler done to return to profitability?

A. They have streamlined their organization by eliminating a large number of employees they didn't need in the first place. They haven't done anything that couldn't have been done five years ago. The upper echelon is still overmanned.

Q. When do you think the price of stock will return to at least twenty-five dollars per share?

A. By changing top management I believe it could reach thirty dollars by the end of 1976.

Q. When you speak of the upper echelon, whom are you referring to?

A. All staff operations above plant manager.

Q. Do plant managers have the power to run their plants?

A. No! Although they are told to run their plant the way they would if it belonged to them, general plants managers and vice presidents really control the activity of a plant. However, when the plant manager is not capable this assistance is necessary.

Q. You seem to have a chip on your shoulder with regard to corporate staffs. Do you?

A. Not really. There are many excellent men on our corporate staffs; however, there are many more than we need, including vice presidents—also, they are overpaid in comparison with plant executives grades twelve through eighteen. A check with our competitors will confirm this.

Q. Do you think Chrysler employees produce as well as Ford or General Motors employees?

A. They are all human beings, just provide them with the facilities and management.

Q. How is the supervisory morale in Chrysler plants?

A. Thinning the ranks, taking away the cost-of-living allowance, and stopping the thrift-stock plan dropped the morale to a very low point. I am sure this action was prompted by drastic necessity.

Q. Is the advertising of Chrysler products adequate?

A. I am sure enough money is spent. We don't appear to be attracting the foreign-car buyers.

Q. Should Chrysler continue to try to meet the international competition?

A. Yes, but in a limited way in countries where we have lost a great deal of money.

Q. What do you think of Chrysler quality?

A. Chrysler goes to great expense to produce and finish products for the comsumer. Warranty costs are expensive. So quality gets the priority. In spite of all the precautions, with the human element involved there still are some defects. Automobiles are built on production assembly lines. There is no such thing as the perfect car coming off any automobile company assembly line.

Q. How soon do you think Chrysler will get back to market penetration of 17 percent or more?

A. As soon as we announce some reorganization of top management. Consumer and public confidence will return to a point where penetration will improve.

Q. Are you and your family still loyal to Chrysler products?

A. You bet! Chrysler builds the best six-cylinder engine on the market. Our market penetration on compacts proves that.

Q. Can Chrysler improve its purchasing methods?

A. Yes! My book states that we scrapped new tools to adjust the inventory value. The purchasing department should be working closely with the plants with regard to tool and machine vendors. Sometimes the cheapest tools and equipment are the most expensive when the results are priced out. We need the right tools when we need them, not a crib full of tools we can't use.

Q. With the recent report of a million-dollar theft ring, what do you think of plant security?

A. It's no credit to the head of the security department. I am sure changes will be made to tighten up the system. It won't be easy to stop completely but improvements could be made. I think every automobile company has problems of this type.

Q. Please explain your emphasis on the need of a good forge and foundry expert.

A. Our forge and foundry divisions in no way compare with our competitors'. Chrysler could well afford to pay some expert $150,000 per year, even if they had to go to Ford or General Motors to get him, and save millions of dollars.

Q. With whom would you replace the top officers?

A. I have never said that all the top officers should be replaced. The company should be headed by automobile manufacturing men, not accountants or industrial engineers. I am sure there are plenty of eager men waiting for this opportunity.

Q. Whom would you replace on the board of directors?

A. Room should be made for an expert on marketing and sales, a product engineering expert, and a public relations expert.

Q. In your book you are very critical about the distribution of incentive compensation. How would you handle the distribution?

A. Well, I wouldn't have four of Chrysler's biggest vendors on the incentive compensation committee. Our top officers should be paid according to profits made per sales dollar. Comparing profits per sales dollars of our competitors, for 1972 and 1973 our top officers were overpaid; paying out so much to so few left very little for plant level executives. We are a company in competition with Ford and General Motors; since they were successful and Chrysler was not, we should learn something by following their pattern. Our plant executives should be compensated the same as our competitors. Our vice president of personnel most likely already knows all the details. Maybe the plant bonus-roll executives would be a more determined staff, if they knew they would get their fair share of the pot.

Q. What do you think of the stock option?

A. Words cannot describe what I think—it is impossible for me to understand. Chrysler cut out the cost-of-living allowance, eliminated the thrift-stock plan, cut executive salaries; then on January 16, 1975, the stock option committee granted options of 420,500 shares at $8.82 per share to the top officers and key men. Nothing was done for the key executives in the plant.

Q. What do you think of the rebate plan to improve sales?

A. Building cars on premium time and selling them at a discount does not sound like good management to me.

Q. What do you consider the difference in top management of the big three?

A. General Motors & Ford elect their top officers on the basis of a long history of outstanding success in the automobile business. There is strong competition to get to the top spot. Chrysler's top management always strikes me as one big happy family.

Q. You refer in your book to an article in *Fortune* magazine. Do you agree with this article?

A. Not all of it. They refer to Chrysler management as being all bad. Chrysler has some excellent managers.

Q. If Chrysler management is so bad, how do these people get such a large percentage of the vote to reelect them?

A. I was very surprised at the announced results of the vote at the meeting of shareholders, who claimed to be representing millions of shares. In view of such a poor management performance, it is all the more surprising.

Q. Do you believe the vote tabulation was legitimate?

A. While it was hard for me to believe, I have no information or proof to the contrary.

Q. At the stockholders' meeting in April, didn't the chairman state that the first quarter would be an improvement over the fourth quarter?

A. Yes, I taped the entire meeting. He said there would be a loss, but it would not be as bad as the fourth quarter of 1974. He was wrong by $30 or $40 million.

Q. Are you of the opinion the labor-relations departments have deteriorated?

A. Definitely! Chrysler has paid out millions of dollars with nothing in return. We have some very unqualified and inexperienced personnel managers and labor relations representatives on both plant and corporate staffs. Very few have any practical experience out in the plants where the money has to be made and the labor problems originate.

Q. Are you of the opinion that the top management should be automobile building and marketing experts?

A. No—although it would help. They must be capable of surrounding themselves with men who have knowledge they themselves lack. With all the square pegs we have in round holes, top management has failed at Chrysler.

Q. Do you really think this book will motivate the shareholders?

A. Yes! Shareholders have a reason to be very unhappy. The big drop in stock value and no dividends should have at least 60 percent of them determined to take action.

Q. What do you think of the recent reorganization at the top level?

A. The appointment of additional executive vice presidents adds to the cost of this overpaid executive group. It makes as much sense as losing $52 million in a record sales year.

Q. With the present chairman retiring the first of

October 1975, do you think this move will help or hurt Chrysler.

A. The two executives who are moving up as a result of his retirement were in high positions last year. Just changing chairs and increasing their salaries won't give the corporation the leadership it so desperately needs.

Summary

The corporation will rise or fall according to the way the nation's economy goes, but it hasn't been—and I don't believe it will be—competitive under the present leadership. Ford Motor Company just announced another sixty-cent dividend payable September 2—they lost money in the first quarter but they are still paying quarterly sixty-cent dividends.

Shareholders at Chrylser have got to unite to save this great corporation from self-destruction by mismanagement. When we elect executives who can run an automobile company and a board of directors that can direct them, Chrysler will become conpetitive. Shareholders will receive a return on their investment. Improved working conditions and higher employment will become a reality. Hope and confidence will replace gloom and despair. These good things rest with the shareholders and the action they choose to take.

Mismanagement in 1974 lost much more than $52 million. The desperation moves top management made in November and December of 1974 lowered morale and created poor attitudes among most of the working force, both hourly and salaried. Drastic changes must be made in upper management before high morale and proper attitudes are reestablished. Productivity and quality will suffer until we have a top-level management team that can generate the confidence and respect of shareholders, employees, consumers, and the general public.